Modern Risk Management in Business

2nd Edition

NAHK RARSI

2ⁿᵈ Edition July 2024

Copyright © 2024 and all rights reserved by

NAHK RARSI and Fixing Knowledge

DEDICATED

To my family, friends, colleagues and students who have always supported me in all phases of my life

ABOUT THE AUTHOR

An Entrepreneur, Philanthropist, Researcher, Professor, Lecturer, Author, Inspirational Motivational and Professional Industrial speaker, having a total of 25+ years of experience in various professional fields.

A person who loves to donate time, experience, skills and talent to help creating a better world.

Passion for demystifying complex technical concepts led me to write books on computers, management and business topics. I have also written books on other genres for modern era.

Enjoy mentoring aspiring leaders, creating videos and teaching on YouTube channel, writing on social media and speaking at technology conferences around the world.

https://nahkrarsi.wordpress.com/

CONTENTS

1 Introduction — Pg 1

2 Fundamentals of Risk Management — Pg 3

    a. Definition of Risk and Risk Management
        i. Define Risk
        ii. Define Risk Management
    b. History and Evolution of Risk Management
        i. Early Risk Management Practices
        ii. Modern Developments
    c. Risk Management Process
    d. Benefits of Risk Management
    e. Types of Risks
        i. Strategic Risks
        ii. Operational Risks
        iii. Financial Risks
        iv. Compliance Risks
        v. Security and Fraud Risks
        vi. Reputational Risks

3 Risk Identification and Assessment — Pg 15

    a. Risk Identification Techniques
        i. SWOT Analysis
        ii. PESTLE Analysis
        iii. Brainstorming
        iv. Scenario Analysis
        v. Bow-Tie Analysis
        vi. Risk Checklists
        vii. Interviews and Surveys
    b. Risk Assessment Methods
        i. Qualitative Risk Assessment
        ii. Quantitative Risk Assessment
        iii. Risk Heat Maps
        iv. Probability and Impact Matrix
        v. Leveraging Technology and Data

4 Risk Mitigation Strategies — Pg 36

    a. Risk Acceptance
    b. Risk Avoidance

       c. Risk Transfer
       d. Risk Reduction
       e. Risk Sharing
       f. Risk Buffering
       g. Risk Strategizing
       h. Risk Testing
       i. Risk Quantification
       j. Risk Digitization
       k. Risk Diversification
       l. Implementing Controls and Safeguards

5 Risk Monitoring and Reporting   Pg 50

       a. Establishing Key Risk Indicators (KRIs)
       b. Risk Dashboards
       c. Incident Reporting Systems
       d. Continuous Monitoring and Auditing
       e. Trend Analysis

6 Financial Risk Management   Pg 58

       a. Credit Risk
       b. Market Risk
       c. Liquidity Risk
       d. Operational Risk
       e. Hedging and Derivatives

7 Enterprise Risk Management (ERM)   Pg 68

       a. ERM Frameworks
           i. COSO ERM Framework
           ii. ISO 31000 Risk Management Standard
           iii. RIMS Risk Maturity Model
       b. Integrating ERM into Business Strategy
       c. Governance and Leadership in ERM
       d. Building a Risk-Aware Culture
       e. Risk Appetite and Tolerance

8 Regulatory and Compliance Risk   Pg 78

       a. Understanding Regulatory Requirements
       b. Compliance Programs
       c. Internal Audits

        d.   Anti-Money Laundering (AML)
        e.   Data Protection and Privacy Regulations

9   Technology and Cyber Risk   Pg 88

        a.   Cybersecurity Threats and Vulnerabilities
        b.   Data Breach Response
        c.   Cyber Risk Assessment and Management
        d.   Role of IT in Risk Management
        e.   Emerging Technologies

10   Operational Risk Management   Pg 99

        a.   Business Continuity Planning
        b.   Disaster Recovery Planning
        c.   Crisis Management
        d.   Supply Chain Risk Management

11   Strategic Risk Management   Pg 107

        a.   Scenario Planning
        b.   Competitive Risk Analysis
        c.   Mergers and Acquisitions Risk
        d.   Innovation and Risk

12   Reputation Risk Management   Pg 116

        a.   Media and Public Relations
        b.   Stakeholder Engagement
        c.   Crisis Communication Plans
        d.   Social Media Risk

13   Risk Management Tools and Software   Pg 123

        a.   Risk Management Information Systems (RMIS)
        b.   Predictive Analytics
        c.   Software for Risk Assessment and Monitoring

14   Case Studies   Pg 131

        a.   Walmart's ERM Framework
        b.   Statoil's ERM Maturity
        c.   Lego: Evolving ERM Over Four Phases
        d.   eBay India's Risk Assessment

  e. Enterprise Risk Management at Intuit
  f. Risk Management Failures at General Motors
  g. Risk Management Failures at Toyota
  h. Lululemon's Yoga Pants Recall
  i. Crowdsourcing to Reduce Movie-Making Risk
  j. Integrating Technology and Data Analytics

15 Best Practices   Pg 143
  a. Conduct Regular Risk Assessments
  b. Quantify and Prioritize Risks
  c. Implement Risk Mitigation Measures
  d. Foster a Risk-Aware Culture
  e. Develop a Comprehensive Risk Management Plan
  f. Regularly Review and Update Strategies
  g. Engage All Stakeholders
  h. Leverage Technology
  i. Leverage Existing Frameworks and Best Practices
  j. Implement Minimum Viable Product (MVP) Development
  k. Conduct Contingency Planning
  l. Perform Root Cause Analysis and Document Lessons Learned
  m. Stay Informed About Risks and Trends
  n. Communicate Effectively
  o. Prioritize and Assess Risks
  p. Implement a Quality Assurance Program
  q. Leverage Data and Analytics
  r. Collaborate Across Functions
  s. Conduct Scenario Planning
  t. Continuously Improve and Adapt

16 Cheat Book   Pg 179

1 INTRODUCTION

Modern risk management in business involves a comprehensive and proactive approach to identifying, assessing, and mitigating various risks that an organization may face.

It goes beyond traditional financial risk management and encompasses a wide range of potential threats, including operational, strategic, compliance, and reputational risks.

We can also say that, modern risk management in business is a holistic and integrated process that aims to protect an organization's assets, reputation, and long-term viability.

It involves the following key elements:

a. Enterprise-wide Risk Identification:

   Organizations systematically identify and categorize potential risks across all areas of their operations, including financial, operational, strategic, legal, and reputational risks.

b. Risk Assessment and Prioritization:

   Risks are evaluated based on their likelihood of occurrence and potential impact, allowing organizations to prioritize and allocate resources effectively.

c. Risk Mitigation Strategies:

   Organizations develop and implement strategies to mitigate or minimize the impact of identified risks. These strategies may include risk avoidance, risk transfer (e.g., insurance), risk reduction, or risk acceptance.

d. Continuous Monitoring and Reporting:

Risk management is an ongoing process that involves continuous monitoring of risk factors, performance indicators, and the effectiveness of mitigation strategies. Regular reporting and communication ensure transparency and accountability.

e. Integration with Strategic Planning:

Modern risk management is closely integrated with an organization's strategic planning process, ensuring that risk considerations are factored into decision-making and long-term objectives.

2 FUNDAMENTALS OF RISK MANAGEMENT

Fundamentals of Risk Management is a comprehensive guide that covers the core principles and frameworks for effective risk management in modern businesses.

a. Definition of Risk and Risk Management
    i. Define Risk
        Risk is defined as the effect of uncertainty on objectives, which can have both positive and negative impacts.

    ii. Define Risk Management
        Risk management is a structured approach to identifying, assessing, and controlling risks that may affect an organization's ability to achieve its objectives.

Risk is inherent in all activities and cannot be fully eliminated. Risks can arise from various sources, including hazards, operational issues, strategic decisions, and external factors. Effective risk management involves understanding the nature of risks, their potential impacts, and the likelihood of their occurrence.

b. History and Evolution of Risk Management
    i. Early Risk Management Practices
        Early risk management practices in business can be traced back to ancient civilizations, where risk transfer and pooling were employed to mitigate risks associated with trade and commerce.

        Ancient Civilizations:
        In ancient times, risk management practices were primarily focused on risk transfer and pooling mechanisms.

For example:
- Babylonian traders used a system of loans to transfer the risk of losing goods during long trade journeys.
- Chinese merchants formed guilds to pool resources and share risks associated with trade caravans.

Medieval and Renaissance Periods

During the medieval and Renaissance periods, risk management practices became more formalized, particularly in the areas of maritime trade and insurance:
- The concept of marine insurance emerged in the 14th century, allowing merchants to transfer the risk of cargo loss to insurers.
- Guilds and associations were formed to pool resources and share risks among members.

Industrial Revolution

The Industrial Revolution brought about significant changes in risk management practices, driven by the growth of large corporations and the need to manage risks associated with new technologies and complex operations:
- The concept of liability insurance emerged to protect businesses from legal risks.
- Risk management became more systematic, with the development of techniques like risk assessment and risk mitigation strategies.

20th Century

In the 20th century, risk management evolved into a more structured discipline, with the introduction of new theories and frameworks:

The concept of enterprise risk management (ERM) emerged, emphasizing a holistic approach to managing risks across an organization.

Quantitative risk analysis techniques, such as value-at-risk (VaR) and stress testing, were developed to measure and manage financial risks.

ii. Modern Developments

The modern concept of risk management evolved gradually over time, transitioning from traditional to more holistic approaches.

Modern Era

In the modern era, risk management practices have been significantly influenced by technological advancements, regulatory changes, and globalization:
- The use of data analytics, artificial intelligence, and machine learning has enabled more sophisticated risk identification and monitoring.
- Increased regulatory requirements, such as Basel III and Sarbanes-Oxley Act, have driven the adoption of more robust risk management frameworks.
- The globalization of businesses has necessitated the management of risks associated with international operations, such as political risks and currency fluctuations.

Overall, the evolution of risk management practices has been driven by the need to adapt to changing business environments, technological advancements, and the increasing complexity of risks faced by organizations.

c. Risk Management Process

The risk management process typically involves the following steps:

i. Establishing the Context:

Defining the scope, objectives, and criteria for risk management.

ii. Risk Identification:
Identifying potential risks that could affect the achievement of objectives.
iii. Risk Analysis:
Analyzing the identified risks to understand their nature, causes, and potential consequences.
iv. Risk Evaluation:
Evaluating the risks based on established criteria to determine their priority and the need for treatment.
v. Risk Treatment:
Selecting and implementing appropriate risk treatment options, such as avoiding, mitigating, transferring, or accepting risks.
vi. Monitoring and Review:
Continuously monitoring and reviewing risks, controls, and the effectiveness of the risk management process.

d. Benefits of Risk Management
Effective risk management can provide numerous benefits to organizations like
  i. Improved decision-making and strategic planning:
  Integrating risk management into strategic planning provides several key benefits that improve decision-making and strategic planning:
    1. Better-informed decisions:
    By identifying and assessing potential risks during the strategic planning process, organizations can make more informed decisions that account for uncertainties and potential obstacles. This allows them to develop strategies that are both ambitious and practical.
    2. Optimized resource allocation:
    Understanding the risks associated with each strategic initiative enables organizations to prioritize resources and focus on areas with the greatest impact. This leads to more efficient use of resources and a higher likelihood of

achieving objectives.
3. Enhanced organizational agility:
   Regularly monitoring and reviewing risks as part of the strategic planning cycle allows organizations to quickly adapt to changing circumstances. This agility is crucial in today's dynamic business environment.
4. Improved achievement of strategic objectives:
   Ultimately, integrating risk management into strategic planning increases the probability of successfully achieving organizational goals. By proactively identifying and mitigating risks, businesses can minimize the impact of adverse events and capitalize on opportunities.
5. Increased resilience:
   By considering risks during goal setting and strategy development, organizations become more resilient to unexpected challenges. This enhances their ability to withstand and recover from setbacks, ensuring long-term success.

ii. Enhanced stakeholder confidence and trust.
Implementing an effective risk management system can significantly enhance stakeholder confidence and trust in several ways:
1. Transparency and communication:
   By regularly communicating risks, mitigation strategies, and performance to stakeholders, organizations demonstrate transparency and accountability. This openness builds trust and confidence.
2. Proactive risk management:
   When stakeholders see that an organization is proactively identifying, assessing, and managing risks, it instills confidence in the company's ability to navigate challenges and protect stakeholder interests.
3. Reduced financial losses:
   Effective risk management helps organizations avoid or

minimize financial losses from potential threats. This financial stability and resilience reassure stakeholders about the company's long-term viability.
4. Preserved brand reputation:
By having a risk management plan that includes guidelines on ethical conduct, public communications, and crisis response, organizations can better protect their brand image and reputation. This brand trust is valuable to stakeholders.
5. Improved decision-making:
Risk management tools like scenario analysis and Monte Carlo simulations help leaders make more informed, high-quality decisions that balance risks and benefits for all stakeholders.
6. Shared responsibility:
Engaging stakeholders in the risk management process fosters a culture of shared responsibility. When stakeholders feel their input is valued, it strengthens their commitment and trust in the organization.

In summary, by communicating transparently, managing risks proactively, preserving financial stability and reputation, and involving stakeholders, organizations can significantly enhance stakeholder confidence and trust through effective risk management practices.

iii. Compliance with legal and regulatory requirements.
Integrating risk management practices can provide significant benefits in ensuring compliance with legal and regulatory requirements. Here are some key ways risk management contributes to compliance:
1. Proactive Risk Identification
By conducting thorough risk assessments, organizations can proactively identify potential compliance risks before they materialize. This allows them to put appropriate

controls and mitigation measures in place to prevent violations and ensure ongoing adherence to laws and regulations.

2. Streamlined Processes

   Effective risk management often involves mapping out processes and establishing clear roles and responsibilities. This helps organizations create efficient, standardized procedures that align with compliance requirements. Automation can further enhance process efficiency and accuracy.

3. Continuous Monitoring

   Risk management frameworks emphasize the importance of ongoing monitoring and review. By continuously tracking compliance indicators and auditing processes, organizations can quickly identify and address any deviations or emerging compliance issues.

4. Reduced Penalties and Fines

   Non-compliance can result in hefty fines, penalties, and legal liabilities. By proactively managing compliance risks, organizations can avoid these costly consequences and protect their financial stability and reputation.

5. Enhanced Reputation

   Demonstrating a strong commitment to compliance through robust risk management practices can enhance an organization's credibility and reputation among customers, partners, and regulators. This can lead to increased trust, loyalty, and business opportunities.

6. Organizational Resilience

   Integrating compliance into overall risk management strategies helps organizations build resilience. By anticipating and mitigating compliance risks, they are better equipped to navigate changing regulatory landscapes and continue operating effectively.

In summary, by identifying, assessing, and managing compliance risks as part of their overall risk management approach, organizations can reap significant benefits in terms of efficiency, cost savings, reputation, and long-term sustainability.

iv. Improved operational efficiency and effectiveness.

Effective operational risk management provides numerous benefits that can improve a company's operational efficiency and effectiveness:

1. Streamlined processes and reduced redundancies:
   By identifying and addressing operational risks, businesses can optimize their processes, eliminate unnecessary steps, and improve overall workflow efficiency.
2. Proactive risk mitigation:
   Implementing a risk management system allows companies to identify potential issues early on and take preventive measures, reducing the likelihood of costly disruptions.
3. Better informed decision-making:
   Operational risk management provides valuable data and insights that enable managers to make more informed decisions about resource allocation, process improvements, and strategic initiatives.
4. Reduced losses and costs:
   Effective risk management helps organizations avoid or minimize the financial impact of operational failures, fraud, and other adverse events, ultimately improving profitability.
5. Improved compliance and regulatory adherence:
   By identifying and addressing risks related to regulatory changes and compliance requirements, companies can avoid penalties and maintain a strong reputation.
6. Enhanced business continuity and resilience:

Robust risk management strategies, such as disaster recovery plans and contingency measures, help organizations maintain operations and bounce back quickly from disruptions.
7. Competitive advantage:
Organizations that effectively manage operational risks can gain a competitive edge by demonstrating their reliability, stability, and ability to adapt to changing market conditions.

By prioritizing operational risk management and embedding it into their culture and processes, companies can enhance their efficiency, effectiveness, and overall competitiveness in the market.

v. Protection of assets and resources.
Risk management has several key benefits that contribute to the protection of assets and resources:
1. Informed decision-making:
By identifying and analyzing potential risks, risk management provides a clearer view of threats and opportunities. This allows leaders to make more informed decisions that minimize risks and maximize returns, leading to better protection of assets.
2. Loss reduction:
One of the main goals of risk management is to minimize financial losses. By proactively identifying and mitigating risks, companies can avoid disastrous situations and protect their financial assets, particularly important in times of economic uncertainty.
3. Compliance with regulations:
Many industries have strict regulations, and non-compliance can result in severe penalties. Risk management helps ensure compliance with relevant regulations, reducing exposure to fines and sanctions that

could threaten assets.
4. Continuous improvement:
Risk management drives continuous improvements by identifying risk areas. Companies can then improve processes, systems, and practices, becoming more efficient and competitive, which protects their assets in the long run.
5. Building trust:
Risk management demonstrates a company's commitment to responsibility and sustainability. This builds trust with investors and customers, strengthening the organization's reputation, which is a valuable asset in itself.
6. Safeguarding personal assets:
Asset protection strategies like setting up proper business entities (e.g. LLCs, corporations) can shield personal assets from liabilities incurred by the business, as long as the separation of business and personal assets is maintained.
7. Protecting business assets:
Business insurance is crucial to safeguard company assets, as a single catastrophic event or lawsuit can be devastating. Proper insurance coverage is vital from the moment a business is established.

In summary, risk management provides a comprehensive approach to identifying, analyzing, and mitigating potential risks. By employing various techniques like diversification, hedging, and asset allocation, investors can protect their assets and resources while still pursuing potential returns

By implementing a comprehensive risk management program aligned with industry best practices and standards, organizations can proactively identify, assess, and manage risks, ultimately supporting the achievement of their objectives and long-term success.

e. Types of Risks
   i. Strategic Risks
      Strategic risk relates to issues that could affect a company's ability to execute its strategic objectives and reach its business goals. This includes risks to the organization's competitive advantages and internal or external factors that could diminish them.
   ii. Operational Risks
      Operational risk involves anything that could affect a company's ability to run its business operations effectively and efficiently. This encompasses the processes, procedures, policies, people and systems that a company has put in place and ensuring they can withstand adverse events.
   iii. Financial Risks
      Financial risk involves business factors that could affect cash flow, profitability, balance sheets and even an organization's solvency. This includes risks related to market movements, foreign currency exchange rates, commodity price fluctuations, and more.
   iv. Compliance Risks
      Compliance risk relates to the laws and regulations that apply to a business. As the legal landscape is constantly evolving, companies need to stay on top of changes in areas like occupational health and safety, taxes, data privacy, and more to avoid penalties.
   v. Security and fraud risk
      Security and fraud risks include data breaches, cyberattacks, identity theft, embezzlement, money laundering, and intellectual property theft. These risks are growing as more business is conducted online and remotely.
   vi. Reputational risk
      Reputational risk involves anything that could negatively impact a company's public image, such as faulty products, poor customer service, negative publicity about employees or leadership, or high-profile failures.

To manage these risks, organizations should identify and prioritize the risks they face, implement prevention measures, and consider insurance where appropriate. Appointing a risk management committee and creating a culture of risk awareness are also key.

3 RISK IDENTIFICATION AND ASSESSMENT

Risk identification and assessment are critical first steps in effective risk management for modern businesses. Risk identification and assessment are critical components of modern risk management for businesses.

The process involves systematically identifying potential risks, analyzing their likelihood and impact, and prioritizing them for further action.

Here are the key points:

- Identifying Risks
  Identifying potential risks is crucial for strategic business planning. Risks can be categorized into physical risks, financial risks, operational risks, compliance risks, strategic risks, and reputational risks. Some techniques for identifying risks include:
  1. Brainstorming sessions with senior managers and employees
  2. SWOT (strengths, weaknesses, opportunities, threats) analysis to identify internal and external factors
  3. Scenario analysis to consider potential future events and their impacts
  4. Consulting a risk library to systematically identify and categorize risks

- Assessing Risks
  Once risks are identified, the next step is to assess them based on likelihood of occurrence and potential impact. This allows prioritizing the most significant risks. Risk assessment techniques include:
  1. Probability analysis using historical data, expert opinions, or statistical methods to estimate likelihood
  2. Impact assessment to evaluate financial and non-financial consequences if a risk occurs

3. Creating a risk matrix and risk register to visualize and prioritize risks
4. Leveraging data analytics, AI and machine learning to process data, identify patterns, and predict risks

- Responding to Risks
  After identifying and assessing risks, organizations can respond by:
  1. Accepting the risk if it is low priority
  2. Transferring the risk through insurance or outsourcing
  3. Reducing the risk by implementing controls and mitigation strategies
  4. Avoiding the risk by not engaging in the risky activity

a. Risk Identification Techniques
   There are several effective risk identification techniques that modern businesses can use to identify and assess potential risks, like
   i. SWOT Analysis
      SWOT (Strengths, Weaknesses, Opportunities, Threats) analysis is a crucial tool for modern risk management in business. It helps organizations identify and analyze their internal strengths and weaknesses, as well as external opportunities and threats, to make informed strategic decisions and effectively manage risks.

      Strengths of SWOT Analysis for Risk Management are
      1. Holistic view:
         SWOT analysis provides a comprehensive understanding of the organization's risk landscape by examining both internal and external factors.
      2. Identification of risks and opportunities:
         By analyzing weaknesses and threats, risk managers can identify current and potential risks. Examining strengths and opportunities helps spot areas for growth and development that can mitigate risks or turn them into advantages.

3. Strategic decision-making:
   SWOT analysis aligns risk management strategies with the organization's strengths and opportunities while addressing its weaknesses and threats, enabling informed, strategic decisions that enhance resilience and competitive advantage.
4. Proactive risk management:
   Continuous monitoring of the internal and external environment through SWOT analysis allows risk managers to anticipate changes and trends that may impact the organization, enabling early detection and mitigation of potential risks.
5. Effective resource allocation:
   Understanding the organization's strengths and weaknesses helps risk managers recommend where to allocate resources to improve resilience and risk preparedness, ensuring efficient and effective use of resources.
6. Enhanced communication and collaboration:
   The SWOT analysis process fosters better communication and collaboration within the organization, providing a structured framework for discussing risks, strategies, and priorities.
7. Adaptability to change:
   SWOT analysis enables regular assessment of how changes in the external environment might impact the organization's risk profile, allowing for quicker adaptation and response to evolving threats and opportunities.

Conducting a SWOT Analysis for Risk Management
1. Define the objective: Clearly define the purpose of the SWOT analysis, such as identifying risks and opportunities related to a specific project, product, or strategic initiative.
2. Gather relevant information: Collect accurate and reliable data about the organization's internal strengths

and weaknesses, as well as external opportunities and threats.
3. Identify and prioritize factors: List and prioritize the most significant strengths, weaknesses, opportunities, and threats relevant to the defined objective.
4. Develop risk management strategies: Use the SWOT analysis insights to develop strategies that leverage strengths, address weaknesses, capitalize on opportunities, and mitigate threats.
5. Implement and monitor: Implement the risk management strategies and continuously monitor the organization's risk profile, updating the SWOT analysis as needed to adapt to changing circumstances.

By integrating SWOT analysis into modern risk management practices, organizations can make more informed decisions, enhance strategic planning, and increase agility and adaptability in the face of evolving risks and opportunities

ii. PESTLE Analysis
PESTLE analysis is a strategic tool used to assess the macro-environmental factors that can impact a business.
It examines the Political, Economic, Social, Technological, Legal, and Environmental influences on an organization.
By analyzing these external factors, businesses can identify potential risks and opportunities, and make informed decisions to mitigate risks and capitalize on opportunities.

Key Components of PESTLE Analysis are
1. Political Factors
Political factors include government policies, political stability, trade regulations, labor laws, and corruption. These factors can significantly impact a business operations, costs, and market access.

2. Economic Factors
   Economic factors such as interest rates, inflation, economic growth, unemployment, and exchange rates can affect a company's purchasing power, pricing, and market supply and demand.
3. Social Factors
   Social factors include demographics, consumer behavior, lifestyle trends, and cultural attitudes. These factors can influence product demand, marketing strategies, and workforce composition.
4. Technological Factors
   Technological factors encompass innovations, research and development, automation, and digital transformation. These factors can impact production processes, communication, and the competitive landscape.
5. Legal Factors
   Legal factors include laws, regulations, and legal changes that can affect a business's operations, such as employment laws, consumer protection laws, and industry-specific regulations.
6. Environmental Factors
   Environmental factors include natural disasters, climate change, sustainability, and environmental regulations. These factors can impact supply chains, operations, and a company's environmental footprint.

Benefits of PESTLE Analysis for Risk Management
1. Anticipating changes:
   PESTLE analysis helps businesses stay informed about upcoming changes in the regulatory environment, allowing them to adapt and mitigate risks.
2. Identifying emerging trends:
   By analyzing external factors, businesses can identify emerging trends and opportunities, enabling them to stay ahead of the competition.

3. Enhancing strategic planning:
   PESTLE analysis provides valuable insights for strategic planning, helping businesses make informed decisions and allocate resources effectively.
4. Assessing market potential:
   PESTLE analysis can help businesses assess the potential of new markets, identifying risks and opportunities before entering.
5. Improving risk management:
   By understanding the macro-environmental factors that can impact a business, PESTLE analysis enables effective risk management strategies

PESTLE analysis is a crucial tool for modern risk management in business. By systematically examining the political, economic, social, technological, legal, and environmental factors, businesses can identify potential risks and opportunities, and make informed decisions to mitigate risks and capitalize on opportunities. Regular PESTLE analysis, combined with other strategic planning tools, can help businesses navigate the complex and ever-changing business environment.

iii. Brainstorming

Brainstorming is a crucial technique for identifying risks in modern business risk management. It involves bringing together a diverse group of individuals, such as senior managers and employees from various departments, to generate a comprehensive list of potential risks facing the organization. The key benefits of using brainstorming for risk identification include:

1. Capturing a wide range of perspectives:
   By involving people with different backgrounds and experiences, brainstorming sessions can uncover risks that may not be obvious to a single individual or department.

2. Encouraging creative thinking:
   The open and collaborative nature of brainstorming stimulates creative thinking and helps participants consider risks from new angles.
3. Fostering team engagement:
   Brainstorming sessions bring people together and encourage collaboration, which can improve team engagement and buy-in for the risk management process.

To conduct an effective brainstorming session for risk identification, follow these steps:
1. Prepare:
   Gather relevant information, such as past risk registers, lessons learned, and industry benchmarks, to inform the discussion.
2. Set the stage:
   Establish clear objectives, ground rules, and a time limit for the session.
3. Encourage participation:
   Create an environment where everyone feels comfortable sharing their ideas without fear of judgment or criticism.
4. Capture ideas:
   Use a facilitator to capture all ideas, even seemingly far-fetched ones, without evaluation or discussion during the brainstorming phase.
5. Categorize and prioritize:
   After the brainstorming session, review and categorize the identified risks based on their likelihood and potential impact.
6. Follow up:
   Assign risk owners, develop mitigation strategies, and monitor the identified risks on an ongoing basis.

By incorporating brainstorming into their risk management process, modern businesses can gain a more comprehensive understanding of their risk landscape and make informed decisions to mitigate potential threats and seize opportunities

iv. Scenario Analysis

Scenario analysis is a crucial tool for modern risk management in business. It involves analyzing the potential impact of various hypothetical scenarios on a company's financial performance, operations, and strategic objectives. In the context of risk management, scenario analysis helps organizations identify and assess risks, evaluate their potential consequences, and develop appropriate mitigation strategies. By considering multiple scenarios, ranging from best-case to worst-case situations, businesses can better understand their exposure to different types of risks and make informed decisions.

However, implementing effective scenario analysis in modern risk management presents several challenges:

1. Data issues:
   Obtaining accurate and relevant data to model scenarios can be difficult, especially when dealing with complex, interconnected risks.
2. Scenario development and management:
   Defining and managing scenarios in a centralized and structured manner is crucial to ensure consistency and traceability.
3. Modeling issues:
   Stress test models used in scenario analysis are forward-looking and often rely on expert judgment, making traditional validation techniques less effective.
4. Governance and control:
   Maintaining effective governance over qualitative adjustments and ensuring consistency across the organization is a key challenge.

To overcome these challenges, organizations can leverage modern technologies such as artificial intelligence (AI) and machine learning (ML) to enhance scenario analysis. AI and ML can help automate data collection, scenario generation, and model validation, reducing reliance on manual interventions and improving efficiency.

Additionally, a well-defined governance framework and centralized management of scenarios and supporting artifacts are essential for effective scenario analysis.

This includes strict controls, versioning, and maintaining historical scenarios for trend analyses and follow-up work.

By embracing modern techniques and technologies, businesses can harness the power of scenario analysis to navigate the complexities of today's risk landscape and make more informed, data-driven decisions.

v. Bow-Tie Analysis

Bow-Tie Analysis is a widely used risk management technique that provides a structured and visual approach to identifying, assessing, and controlling risks in business operations. It combines two existing risk analysis tools - fault trees and event trees - to create a diagram that resembles a bow tie, hence the name.

The Bow-Tie diagram consists of five key elements:
1. Hazard:
   The central event or situation that has the potential to cause harm or loss.
2. Threats or Causes:
   The events or actions that can lead to the occurrence of the hazard.
3. Preventive Controls:
   The barriers or safeguards that are put in place to prevent the threats from causing the hazard.

4. Consequences:
   The potential outcomes or impacts that may result if the hazard occurs.
5. Recovery Controls:
   The measures taken to mitigate or recover from the consequences of the hazard.

The Bow-Tie method offers several benefits for modern risk management in business:
1. Visual representation:
   The diagram provides a clear and easy-to-understand visual representation of the risk, making it accessible to stakeholders at all levels of the organization.
2. Causal relationships:
   The Bow-Tie highlights the causal links between threats, controls, and consequences, enabling a better understanding of the risk landscape.
3. Gap analysis:
   The method facilitates the identification of deficiencies or missing risk controls, allowing for targeted improvements.
4. Alignment with other methodologies:
   Bow-Tie analysis complements and aligns with other risk management frameworks, such as Likelihood and Consequence Management, P2R2, Swiss Cheese, and Root Cause Analysis.
5. Adequacy of controls:
   Existing controls are identified, listed, and linked to specific threats, enabling an assessment of their effectiveness.
6. Scenario modeling:
   Typical scenarios and relationships can be depicted on the left side of the Bow-Tie diagram, aiding in risk identification and assessment.
7. Communication and decision-making:
   The visual nature of the Bow-Tie makes it an effective tool

for communicating risks and supporting management decision-making.

The Bow-Tie method can be applied both qualitatively and quantitatively to assess risks from various hazards. It involves identifying threats, consequences, barriers, and recovery factors, and assessing their effectiveness to control risks.

In summary, Bow-Tie Analysis is a powerful risk management tool that provides a structured and visual approach to identifying, assessing, and controlling risks in modern business operations. Its simplicity, alignment with other methodologies, and ability to facilitate communication and decision-making make it a valuable addition to an organization's risk management toolkit.

vi. Risk Checklist

Risk checklists are an essential tool for modern risk management in business. They provide a structured approach to identifying, assessing, and mitigating potential risks across all aspects of an organization. Here are the key points about risk checklists and their importance in effective risk management:

What are Risk Checklists?

Risk checklists are comprehensive lists of potential risks that a business may face. They serve as a guide to ensure that all possible risk categories are thoroughly evaluated and addressed. These checklists can be tailored to specific industries, business functions, or projects, and are regularly updated to reflect changing risk landscapes.

Benefits of Using Risk Checklists
1. Comprehensive coverage:
    Risk checklists help ensure that no potential risks are

overlooked by systematically evaluating all relevant areas of the business.
2. Consistency:
Using standardized checklists promotes consistency in the risk assessment process, reducing the likelihood of inconsistencies or oversights.
3. Efficiency:
Checklists streamline the risk assessment process by providing a structured framework for gathering and organizing risk-related information, saving time and effort.
4. Accuracy:
Checklists enhance the accuracy of risk assessments by ensuring that all necessary information is captured and analyzed in a systematic manner.

Key Components of Risk Checklists
Effective risk checklists typically include the following components:
1. Risk categories:
Checklists organize potential risks into categories such as financial, operational, legal, reputational, and strategic risks.
2. Risk descriptions:
Each risk is clearly defined and described, including its potential causes and consequences.
3. Risk likelihood and impact:
The probability of each risk occurring and its potential impact on the organization are assessed and documented.
4. Risk mitigation strategies:
Specific actions and controls to mitigate or manage each risk are identified and assigned to responsible parties.
5. Risk monitoring:
Processes for regularly monitoring and updating the risk checklist are established to ensure its ongoing relevance and effectiveness.

Developing and Implementing Risk Checklists

To develop and implement effective risk checklists, organizations should follow these steps:

1. Identify risk categories:
   Determine the key risk categories relevant to the business, industry, and specific projects or functions.
2. Gather input:
   Involve stakeholders, subject matter experts, and risk management professionals in identifying potential risks.
3. Prioritize risks:
   Assess the likelihood and potential impact of each risk to prioritize them for mitigation efforts.
4. Assign risk owners:
   Designate individuals responsible for managing and monitoring specific risks.
5. Regularly review and update:
   Review and update the risk checklists periodically to reflect changes in the business environment, new risks, and the effectiveness of mitigation strategies.

By implementing comprehensive risk checklists as part of a broader risk management strategy, businesses can proactively identify, assess, and mitigate potential risks, enhancing their resilience and ability to seize opportunities in an ever-changing business landscape.

vii. Interviews and Surveys

Interviews and surveys are essential tools for modern risk management in business. They help organizations gather valuable insights and data to identify, assess, and mitigate risks effectively. Here are some key aspects of using interviews and surveys for risk management:

AI-Powered Interviews

AI can standardize interview processes to consistently capture unstructured data, while natural language processing (NLP) makes it easy to sift through interview transcripts and uncover hidden patterns and trends. AI can group and summarize frequently used words and phrases, surfacing critical insights and trends for more informed decision-making.

Risk Surveys: Beyond Checkbox Responses

Traditional risk surveys collect checkbox responses. AI-enhanced surveys go beyond a checkbox approach by:
1. Augmenting surveys with workflow automation for seamless real-time reporting
2. Providing text analysis to extract insights from open-ended survey responses
3. Identifying custom risk factors unique to each organization
4. Triggering instant visualizations based on predefined thresholds and weights

Interviews and Surveys in Risk Assessments

Interviews and surveys are crucial components of risk assessments. They help organizations gather data on risk perceptions, risk appetite, and risk management practices from various stakeholders.

The skills deemed most important when recruiting new candidates for technology risk roles are a combination of technical and business experience (72%) and prior risk management experience (66%). Specific technical experience (49%) and a problem-solving 'agile' mindset (46%) are also increasingly important.

Challenges and Opportunities

While interviews and surveys provide valuable insights, they also present challenges. Ensuring consistent and unbiased data collection, managing language barriers, and effectively communicating risk-related information are some of the key challenges.

However, AI-powered tools can help mitigate these challenges by enhancing communication impact, facilitating continuous risk management, and democratizing data and analytics within organizations.

By leveraging interviews and surveys in conjunction with AI and data analytics, organizations can gain a comprehensive understanding of their risk landscape, make more informed decisions, and proactively manage risks in today's dynamic business environment.

b. Risk Assessment Methods
  i. Qualitative Risk Assessment
     Qualitative risk assessment is an important tool for modern risk management in business. It involves subjective evaluation of risks based on expert judgment and experience rather than numerical data.

     Here are the key points about qualitative risk assessment:
     1. Qualitative risk assessment categorizes risks into broad groupings like high, medium, or low based on the likelihood and impact of potential risk events. This provides a general picture of the organization's risk landscape.
     2. It is easier and less labor-intensive to implement compared to quantitative methods. Assessors use their industry expertise and knowledge of the business to analyze risks.
     3. Qualitative assessment helps prioritize risks, identify main risk exposures, and understand relationships between risks. This allows focusing risk management efforts on the most critical areas.

4. However, qualitative assessments are subjective and open to interpretation. The accuracy depends heavily on the assessors' experience and can be affected by bias.
5. To address this, some organizations use a semi-quantitative approach, assigning numerical risk scores that are then categorized as low, medium or high. This provides more objectivity.
6. Qualitative assessment is often combined with quantitative methods to get a more comprehensive view of risks. Quantitative analysis provides more precise estimates of risk probabilities and impacts.

In summary, qualitative risk assessment is a valuable tool for modern businesses to gain a general understanding of their risk profile and prioritize risk management efforts. However, it should be used in conjunction with quantitative methods for a more complete risk picture.

ii. Quantitative Risk Assessment

Quantitative risk assessment is a critical tool for modern risk management in business. It leverages numerical values and calculations to identify, measure, and manage potential risks associated with a given project or decision.

Key advantages of quantitative risk assessment include:
1. Providing numeric data to facilitate objective decision-making
2. Helping prioritizes risks based on probability and impact
3. Enabling financial planning by associating monetary values with risks
4. Enhancing communication of risk exposure to stakeholders
5. Supporting continuous risk monitoring

The quantitative approach involves several steps:
1. Identifying risks the business is exposed to
2. Analyzing the scope and severity of each risk

3. Evaluating and ranking risks based on likelihood and impact
4. Treating high-priority risks through mitigation strategies
5. Monitoring risks and reviewing the assessment process

Quantitative risk assessment relies on accurate statistical data to produce actionable insights. It assigns numerical probabilities to risks and quantifies their potential impact on cost, schedule, resources, etc. This allows setting achievable targets and assessing the likelihood of achieving objectives. While more complex than qualitative methods, quantitative risk assessment is considered more objective and better suited for large, high-risk projects. It provides the robust analysis needed to make well-informed decisions and successfully execute projects

iii. Risk Heat Maps
Risk heat maps are a widely used tool for visualizing and managing organizational risks. They provide a concise, at-a-glance view of potential threats by plotting risks along axes of likelihood and impact.

Key benefits of risk heat maps include:
1. Intuitive visual representation that enables quick identification and prioritization of risks
2. Color-coding and size variations distinguish between different levels of impact and likelihood, supporting efficient resource allocation
3. Holistic view of risk interplay, considering both immediate and long-term consequences for more nuanced decision-making

To create an effective risk heat map:
1. Identify and categorize potential risks through thorough assessments, data analysis, and stakeholder engagement

2. Evaluate each risk's likelihood and potential impact, assigning appropriate ratings
3. Plot risks on the heat map, typically using a "stoplight" color scheme (green=low, yellow=medium, red=high risk)
4. Calculate each risk's score using the formula: Risk = Potential Impact × Probability of Occurrence

Advanced practices include:
1. Incorporating control effectiveness as a third dimension, showing how well controls mitigate risks
2. Considering additional factors like velocity (speed of onset), acceptability, and external context for a more robust framework.

To keep the heat map current, risks should be reviewed periodically and discussed with stakeholders at least quarterly. Involving employees at all levels helps create a risk-aware culture and improves the map's accuracy.

By adopting risk heat maps and modern best practices, organizations can transform traditional risk management into a dynamic, proactive process that protects and enhances strategic decision-making

iv. Probability and Impact Matrix

The Probability and Impact Matrix is a widely used tool in modern risk management to assess and prioritize risks in business. It helps organizations evaluate the potential consequences (impact) of a risk and the likelihood (probability) of that risk occurring.

Here's how it works:
1. Probability:
    This measures the likelihood or chance that a specific risk event will occur, often expressed as a percentage or qualitative assessment (e.g., low, medium, high).

2. Impact:
   This measures the severity of the consequences or effects if the risk event were to occur. Impact can be assessed on various dimensions, such as financial, operational, reputational, or safety, and is also often expressed qualitatively (e.g., low, medium, high).
3. Matrix:
   The matrix is a two-dimensional grid or table where the probability and impact of each identified risk are plotted. It typically contains rows and columns, with probability levels on one axis (e.g., low, medium, high) and impact levels on the other axis (e.g., low, medium, high).

By placing each risk into the matrix based on its estimated probability and impact, risks can be categorized into different risk zones:
1. High Probability, High Impact:
   Risks in this quadrant are the most critical and require immediate attention and mitigation.
2. High Probability, Low Impact:
   These risks are likely to occur but may have relatively minor consequences.
3. Low Probability, High Impact:
   These risks have the potential for severe consequences but are less likely to occur.
4. Low Probability, Low Impact:
   Risks in this quadrant have a low likelihood of occurring and would have minimal consequences if they did.

Once the risks are categorized, organizations can focus their efforts on addressing and mitigating high-priority risks, ensuring that resources are allocated effectively to manage potential issues and opportunities. The Probability and Impact Matrix is a valuable tool for risk assessment, decision-making, and strategic planning in modern business risk management

v. Leveraging Technology and Data

Leveraging technology and data is crucial for modern risk management in business. Here are some key methods to enhance risk management processes and systems:

1. Identify and assess risks more effectively and efficiently using artificial intelligence (AI), machine learning (ML), natural language processing (NLP), and sentiment analysis to detect patterns, anomalies, and trends in large amounts of data from various sources. Simulation and scenario analysis can also model the impact and likelihood of different risk events.
2. Monitor and control risks more proactively and dynamically by continuously tracking and measuring risk management performance using real-time monitoring systems. This allows for prompt identification of emerging risks.
3. Improve risk mitigation strategies through scenario analysis to assess the effectiveness of different mitigation approaches, optimization models to allocate resources, and tailored responses based on specific risk profiles.
4. Facilitate data-driven decision making by basing decisions on empirical evidence, refining strategies based on data-driven feedback, and enhancing transparency and accountability. Predictive analytics can utilize historical data to forecast future risk scenarios.
5. Leverage artificial intelligence (AI) to propel risk maturity to new heights by scanning large amounts of data to predict risks before they materialize, enabling a proactive stance. AI-driven analytics can uncover insights that were previously unattainable.
6. Ensure data quality is paramount, as risk management is only as good as the data it is based on. Meticulous data verification and effective data management are crucial for accurate risk reporting and informed decision making.

By harnessing the power of technology and data, businesses can transform their risk management from reactive to proactive, making informed decisions aligned with strategic objectives and driving greater resilience and success.

However, this transition requires a well-thought-out strategy encompassing both technological and human aspects of change management.

4 RISK MITIGATION STRATEGIES

Risk mitigation strategies are actions taken to reduce the likelihood or impact of potential risks that could negatively affect a business.

Here are some key risk mitigation strategies for modern businesses:

a. Risk Acceptance
Risk acceptance is a risk mitigation strategy where an organization consciously decides to accept a risk and deal with its consequences if it occurs, rather than trying to avoid or mitigate it. This approach is appropriate when the risk is sufficiently low-impact and the cost of mitigating it outweighs the potential damage.

Some key points about risk acceptance as a modern risk management strategy:
i. It involves acknowledging the risk and being prepared to handle its impact if it materializes. The organization should have a plan for how to respond if the risk event occurs.
ii. Risks are accepted when they are within the organization's risk tolerance level and the potential consequences are manageable. The risk should not be too severe or likely to occur.
iii. Accepting risk allows the organization to focus resources on higher priority risks that require mitigation or avoidance. It's a way to prioritize risks.
iv. It's often used for risks that are unlikely to occur or have a low impact, where the cost of mitigating the risk is disproportionately high compared to the potential damage.
v. Risks that are accepted should be continuously monitored

in case the risk profile changes and mitigation becomes necessary. Periodic risk assessments are important.

In summary, risk acceptance is a valid risk management strategy for modern businesses when used judiciously for low-priority risks. It allows an organization to focus its risk mitigation efforts where they are most needed. But it requires continuous monitoring and a plan for how to handle the risk if it does occur.

b. Risk Avoidance
    Risk avoidance is a key strategy in modern risk management for businesses. It involves completely avoiding activities or situations that carry unacceptable risks. Some examples of risk avoidance include:
    i.   Declining to work with customers who have a history of defaulting on loans to avoid credit risk
    ii. Identifying risks in a project and taking steps to prevent them from occurring, such as avoiding cost overruns by identifying all expected and unexpected costs upfront
    iii. Evacuating employees in advance of a severe storm to minimize potential risks to life

    Risk avoidance is suitable when the potential impact of a risk is high and the cost of mitigating it is also high. It allows businesses to focus their risk mitigation efforts on the most significant threats. However, risk avoidance should be balanced with other risk management strategies. Completely avoiding all risks is often impractical and can hinder business growth. Businesses should carefully evaluate each risk and determine if avoidance is the most appropriate response based on the likelihood, potential consequences, and costs involved. Effective risk avoidance requires a clear risk management framework to consistently identify, assess and prioritize risks. Continuous risk monitoring is also crucial to stay informed about emerging threats and adapt avoidance strategies accordingly. Employee training on risk awareness is another important component.

In summary, risk avoidance is a valuable tool in the modern business risk management toolkit, but it should be applied judiciously as part of a comprehensive risk mitigation strategy that also includes risk acceptance, transfer, sharing and other approaches tailored to each organization's unique risk profile and objectives

c. Risk Transfer

Risk transfer is an essential risk mitigation strategy for modern businesses facing a wide range of potential threats. By transferring risk to another party, businesses can reduce their exposure and financial liability in the event of a negative occurrence.

Some key ways businesses can transfer risk include:
i. Purchasing insurance policies to cover losses from events like data breaches, natural disasters, or lawsuits
ii. Outsourcing high-risk activities to third-party providers with specialized expertise and risk management practices
iii. Entering into contractual agreements that shift liability to other parties, such as suppliers or customers
iv. Using financial instruments like derivatives to hedge against market risks

Risk transfer is particularly useful for risks with a high potential impact that are difficult or costly for the business to mitigate on its own. However, it's important to carefully evaluate the costs and coverage of risk transfer options to ensure they align with the organization's risk tolerance and budget. Risk transfer should be part of a comprehensive risk management framework that also includes strategies like risk avoidance, risk mitigation, and risk acceptance. By combining multiple risk mitigation techniques, modern businesses can build resilience and protect their operations, finances, and reputation in an increasingly complex risk landscape.

d. Risk Reduction

Risk reduction (also known as risk control) involves taking actions to reduce the likelihood of a risk occurring or limit its impact if it does occur. It's a proactive approach to managing risks that businesses face. Some examples of risk reduction strategies include:
   i. Implementing redundant systems or backup plans to minimize the impact of a critical system failure
   ii. Developing contingency plans or alternative strategies to manage risks in smaller segments
   iii. Performing comprehensive risk testing like vulnerability assessments and code reviews to identify and remediate potential issues
   iv. Investing in cybersecurity measures to mitigate the risk of data breaches
   v. Establishing clear agreements and communication channels when sharing risks with partners or third parties

Risk reduction is most appropriate when the likelihood and potential impact of a risk is high. It requires clearly defining risks upfront, proactively tracking them during projects, and monitoring them over time so mitigation actions can be taken if needed.

Effective risk reduction is part of a larger risk management framework that also includes risk identification, assessment, and prioritization. Continuously assessing risks, maintaining risk registers, and conducting regular reviews are key practices to keep risk reduction strategies current and aligned with the evolving risk landscape.

By implementing risk reduction strategies, modern businesses can proactively minimize threats to their operations, finances, and objectives. It's an essential component of a comprehensive risk management program to ensure business continuity and resilience

e. Risk Sharing

Risk sharing is an effective risk mitigation strategy for modern businesses. It involves transferring risk to another party, such as an insurance company or a partner organization, to reduce the financial impact on the business.

Some key aspects of risk sharing include:
i. Purchasing insurance policies to cover potential losses from events like cyber-attacks, natural disasters, or liability claims
ii. Entering into contractual agreements with suppliers, vendors, or customers to share responsibility for risks
iii. Collaborating with other businesses or forming strategic alliances to pool resources and spread risk across multiple parties

By transferring risk to other entities, businesses can:
i. Limit their financial exposure to potential losses
ii. Gain access to specialized expertise and resources for managing certain risks
iii. Improve their ability to withstand unexpected events and maintain business continuity

However, risk sharing should be carefully considered and implemented. Businesses need to evaluate the reliability and financial strength of the parties they are transferring risk to, and ensure that the risk transfer mechanisms are legally binding and enforceable.

Additionally, risk sharing does not eliminate risk entirely; it simply shifts the responsibility for managing and absorbing the risk to another party. Businesses should still maintain robust risk management practices, such as risk assessment, risk monitoring, and contingency planning, to effectively manage the risks they share with others.

In conclusion, risk sharing is a valuable risk mitigation strategy that allows modern businesses to transfer certain risks to other parties, thereby reducing their overall risk exposure and enhancing their resilience in the face of potential threats and uncertainties.

f. Risk Buffering

Risk buffering is an essential risk mitigation strategy that involves adding extra resources, time, or personnel to mitigate the potential impact of a risk. This approach establishes a reserve or buffer that can absorb the effects of many risks without jeopardizing the project or business operations. Some examples of risk buffering include:

   i. Implementing redundant servers or backup systems to reduce the risk of critical system failures
   ii. Maintaining a healthy cash flow that covers salaries for the next few months in case of unexpected events
   iii. Keeping disaster recovery systems or data backups in case of system failures or data breaches

Risk buffering is particularly useful when the potential impact of a risk is high and the cost of mitigating it is significant. By adding extra resources or contingency plans, organizations can reduce the likelihood of a risk event causing major disruptions or financial losses.

However, it's important to strike a balance between risk buffering and cost-effectiveness. Excessive buffering can lead to inefficiencies and unnecessary expenses. Organizations should carefully assess the potential risks, their likelihood, and the cost of mitigation strategies to determine the appropriate level of risk buffering.

In summary, risk buffering is a valuable risk mitigation strategy that involves adding extra resources, time, or personnel to absorb the potential impact of risks.

By implementing redundant systems, maintaining cash reserves, and developing contingency plans, businesses can enhance their resilience and minimize the consequences of unexpected events.

g. Risk Strategizing

Risk strategizing is an essential risk mitigation strategy for modern businesses facing a rapidly evolving risk landscape. It involves creating contingency plans or "Plan B" scenarios to manage specific risks.

Key aspects of risk strategizing include:
  i. Developing alternative strategies to manage projects or operations in smaller, more manageable segments to reduce potential risks
  ii. Establishing clear risk response plans that outline the steps the business will take in the face of each identified risk, ensuring a swift and calculated reaction when necessary
  iii. Maintaining flexibility in risk management approaches to adapt to changing circumstances and emerging threats

By proactively strategizing and planning for potential risks, businesses can:
  i. Minimize the impact of disruptive events on operations and profitability
  ii. Capitalize on opportunities that may arise from managing risks effectively

    iii.   Foster a culture of preparedness and agility within the organization

Risk strategizing should be integrated into the broader business strategy and risk management framework. It should be supported by continuous risk assessment, monitoring, and adaptation to ensure the strategies remain relevant and effective in the face of an evolving risk landscape.

Ultimately, risk strategizing empowers modern businesses to navigate uncertainty with confidence, making them more resilient and better positioned for long-term success.

h. Risk Testing

Risk testing is a crucial risk mitigation strategy for modern businesses to identify and address potential threats. It involves conducting various tests to verify the security and functionality of systems, processes, and projects. Some key aspects of risk testing include:

    i.   Vulnerability assessments to identify security weaknesses that could be exploited by attackers
    ii.   Code reviews to catch bugs and vulnerabilities in software before deployment
    iii.   Penetration testing to simulate real-world attacks and assess an organization's ability to detect and respond to threats
    iv.   Tabletop exercises to test business continuity and disaster recovery plans by walking through hypothetical scenarios

A comprehensive risk testing program should be part of a broader risk management framework that includes risk identification, assessment, and mitigation strategies tailored to the organization's specific risks and risk appetite. Some other effective risk mitigation strategies for modern businesses include:

i. Risk avoidance by eliminating activities with unacceptable risks
ii. Risk transfer through insurance policies or third-party contracts
iii. Risk reduction by implementing controls and safeguards to minimize the likelihood and impact of risks
iv. Risk acceptance for low-impact risks where the cost of mitigation outweighs the potential consequences

Integrating risk management into strategic decision-making, leveraging data analytics, and continuously monitoring and adapting to emerging threats are also key to effective risk management in today's dynamic business environment

i. Risk Quantification

Risk quantification is a critical strategy for modern risk management in business. It involves using statistical methods to communicate the financial impact of risks in objective terms, rather than subjective qualitative assessments. This enables organizations to prioritize risks based on their potential magnitude of loss, leading to better cybersecurity budget allocation, investment decisions, and mitigation strategies.

Key benefits of risk quantification include:
i. Prioritizing risks that pose the greatest financial threat to address first
ii. Revealing strategic risk opportunities to gain competitive advantage
iii. Streamlining risk operations by spending less time on vague "best guess" analyses
iv. Communicating risk posture more clearly to leadership and the board

To effectively implement risk quantification, organizations should:

i. Quantify risks using statistical models to determine potential financial impact
ii. Conduct quantitative risk assessments across the entire risk register to get a full picture of exposure
iii. Communicate risk in numerical, measurable terms to leadership for better understanding and alignment
iv. Leverage risk quantification tools to pull off the art and science of modeling risk outcomes

By accurately quantifying risks, organizations can make more informed decisions about risk transfer through insurance, risk sharing among stakeholders, and prioritizing risk mitigation efforts based on potential impact. This allows for more effective allocation of resources and enhances the safety and security of projects by addressing risks before they escalate.

In summary, risk quantification is an essential strategy for modern businesses to proactively manage risks, make data-driven decisions, and communicate risk in a common language across the organization. Paired with other mitigation techniques like risk reduction, avoidance, transference and acceptance, it forms a comprehensive approach to safeguarding profitability and ensuring business continuity.

j. Risk Digitization
   To effectively mitigate risks in the digital age, businesses should implement a comprehensive risk digitization strategy that includes the following key elements:
   i. Establish a Digital Risk Management Framework
      1. Develop a risk-based digital architecture customized to the organization's needs and operating environment
      2. Implement a continuous review process that evolves in response to disruption and new developments across the digital estate, legal and regulatory requirements

ii. Secure Endpoints and Network Infrastructure
   1. Secure endpoints by controlling and monitoring web access, installing firewalls and antivirus software, and enforcing password security and multi-factor authentication
   2. Reinforce network infrastructure by installing, testing, and layering security programs and implementing multiple security protocols
iii. Leverage Data, Analytics and IT Architecture
   1. Upgrade risk data, establish robust data governance, enhance data quality and metadata, and build the right data architecture
   2. Utilize modern technologies like big data platforms, cloud, machine learning, AI and natural language processing to support risk processes and analytics
iv. Develop Organizational Capabilities
   1. Put in place the right talent and nurture an innovative "test and learn" mindset in the risk function
   2. Establish governance processes that enable nimble responses to a fast-moving technological and regulatory environment
v. Prioritize and Adapt Initiatives
   1. Capture high-value opportunities first when digitizing risk processes
   2. Take a modular approach, adapting test-and-learn pilots to the risk context with robust controls and thorough testing

By implementing these strategies, businesses can effectively mitigate digital risks and ensure the success of their digital transformation initiatives in the modern risk landscape

k. Risk Diversification
Risk diversification is a key strategy for modern businesses to mitigate various types of risks in their operations. By spreading

out potential risks across different projects, products, investments, or business areas, the impact of a failure in any one area is reduced.

Some specific ways businesses can implement risk diversification include:
i. Investing in a mix of stocks, bonds, and alternative assets to balance risk and return
ii. Expanding into new markets and geographic regions to reduce reliance on a single market
iii. Offering a diverse range of products and services to appeal to a broader customer base
iv. Partnering with multiple suppliers and vendors to avoid over-dependence on a single source
v. Allocating resources across different business units and projects to avoid concentration risk

Diversification is most effective when combined with other risk management strategies like continuous risk assessment, incident response planning, and leveraging technology and data analytics.

By taking a holistic approach to risk management, modern businesses can build resilience and adaptability to navigate an increasingly complex and uncertain business landscape.

1. Implementing Controls and Safeguards
   Implementing effective controls and safeguards is a critical risk mitigation strategy for modern businesses. Here are some key elements to consider:
   i. Establishing a Risk Management Framework
      Developing a clear and structured risk management framework is the foundation for implementing robust controls and safeguards. This framework should define the processes and methodologies for identifying, assessing, and mitigating risks consistently across the organization.

ii. Implementing Preventive Controls
Preventive controls aim to reduce the likelihood of risks occurring in the first place. Examples include:
1. Enhanced security protocols like multi-factor authentication and encryption to mitigate cyber threats
2. Redundant systems and backup infrastructure to ensure business continuity in case of failures or disasters
3. Thorough employee screening and training programs to minimize insider risks

iii. Deploying Detective Controls
Detective controls are designed to identify risks that have materialized so they can be addressed quickly. These include:
1. Real-time monitoring systems to detect anomalies and potential threats
2. Regular audits and compliance checks to identify control weaknesses
3. Incident response plans to guide actions when risks manifest

iv. Establishing Corrective Controls
Corrective controls minimize the impact of risks that have occurred and help restore normal operations. Examples include:
1. Incident response and disaster recovery plans
2. Backup and restoration procedures for critical data and systems
3. Processes for remediating control failures and vulnerabilities

v. Continuously Reviewing and Updating Controls
Risk landscapes are constantly evolving, so controls and safeguards must be regularly reviewed and updated to remain effective. This includes:
1. Conducting periodic risk assessments to identify new and changing risks

2. Evaluating the ongoing effectiveness of existing controls
3. Implementing improvements and enhancements based on lessons learned and industry best practices

By implementing a comprehensive set of preventives, detective, and corrective controls, and continuously reviewing and updating them, modern businesses can significantly enhance their resilience and ability to manage risks effectively.

Integrating these controls with a robust risk management framework and a risk-aware culture is key to success.

5 RISK MONITORING AND REPORTING

Risk monitoring and reporting are essential components of modern risk management in business.

Risk monitoring refers to the ongoing process of identifying, assessing, and tracking potential risks that could impact an organization's operations, financial stability, and reputation. It involves collecting, analyzing, and interpreting data on identified risks to produce useful information for decision-making.

Risk reporting is the process of communicating risk-related information to key stakeholders, including management, the board of directors, and regulatory bodies. Effective risk reporting allows organizations to make informed decisions, prioritize risks, and allocate resources to mitigate the most pressing threats.

Key benefits of risk monitoring and reporting include:
i. Increased awareness of risks throughout the organization
ii. Better coordination of compliance strategies with internal and external control mandates
iii. Improved operational efficiency through consistent risk processes and controls
iv. Enhanced workplace safety and security
v. Competitive advantage in the market

To implement effective risk monitoring and reporting, organizations should follow these best practices:
i. Establish clear risk management frameworks and policies that define roles, responsibilities, and risk tolerance levels
ii. Conduct regular risk assessments to identify, analyze, and prioritize risks based on their likelihood and potential impact
iii. Implement risk monitoring systems that collect and analyze data from various sources, such as financial records, operational metrics, and external data feeds

iv. Develop key risk indicators (KRIs) that provide early warning signals of emerging risks and help track the effectiveness of risk mitigation strategies
v. Establish regular risk reporting mechanisms, such as dashboards, scorecards, and risk registers, to communicate risk information to stakeholders
vi. Foster a risk-aware culture by promoting risk management as a shared responsibility across all levels of the organization

a. Establishing Key Risk Indicators (KRIs)

Key Risk Indicators (KRIs) are essential metrics that help organizations identify, assess, and mitigate potential risks that impact their objectives. Establishing effective KRIs is crucial for a robust risk management strategy in today's dynamic business environment.

Here are the key steps to establish KRIs for modern risk management:

i. Understand Your Needs

Clearly understand the organization's objectives, processes, and potential risks for successful KRI risk management.

ii. Gather Information
1. Engage with different departments, conduct surveys, employ effective risk assessment tools, and gather data to understand potential risks better.
2. The more information available for risk assessment, the more precise the organization's risk landscape becomes.

iii. Characteristics of Effective KRIs
1. Quantifiable: Measurable in numbers or percentages.
2. Reliable: The data should be reliable and consistent.
3. Verifiable: There should be a way to verify the accuracy of the KRI.
4. Predictable: They should provide foresight into potential risks.
5. Relevant: They should be directly related to the associated risk.

iv. Map Business Strategy
   1. Define the company's objectives and the processes required to meet those objectives for KRI risk management.
   2. Mapping the business strategy, objectives, and associated risks makes it easier to determine the most relevant key risk indicators.
v. Automation and Real-time Monitoring
   1. Automation plays a pivotal role in monitoring KRIs, enabling real-time evaluation of risk metrics and continuous modification of risk management strategies.
   2. Tools and software can simplify the KRI risk management process, making it more efficient and effective.
vi. Regular Review and Update
   1. Regularly review and update key risk indicators to ensure they remain relevant and effective for identifying potential risks.
   2. The business environment is dynamic, and risks evolve over time.
vii. Stakeholder Engagement
   1. Engage with stakeholders, including employees, management, and external partners, to gather feedback on the KRIs.
   2. Their insights can provide valuable information on the effectiveness of the KRIs and areas for improvement.

By following these steps and incorporating the best practices for developing KRIs, organizations can establish a robust risk management framework that helps them navigate the complex landscape of modern risks and achieve their objectives.

b. Risk Dashboards
Risk dashboards are essential tools for modern risk management in business. They provide a consolidated view of an

organization's risk profile, enabling effective monitoring, analysis, and decision-making.

Here are the key benefits of using risk dashboards for enterprise risk management:

i. Consolidation of data:
Risk dashboards aggregate data from various sources, providing a single view of an organization's risk landscape. This eliminates the need to manually compile information from multiple spreadsheets or systems.

ii. Real-time monitoring:
Dashboards enable real-time monitoring of key risk indicators, allowing organizations to quickly identify and respond to emerging threats. This proactive approach helps mitigate risks before they escalate.

iii. Enhanced decision-making:
By simplifying complex data into easily understandable visualizations, risk dashboards support informed decision-making. They help executives and managers quickly identify high-risk areas and prioritize risk mitigation efforts.

iv. Improved transparency and accountability:
Risk dashboards foster transparency by providing a clear view of an organization's risk profile to stakeholders. This enhances accountability and collaboration in the risk management process.

v. Automation and scalability:
Modern risk management platforms offer dashboards that are easily configurable and scalable. Automation reduces manual effort and ensures consistent, up-to-date reporting, even as the organization's risk profile evolves.

To create effective risk dashboards, organizations should focus on developing a passion for learning, ensuring sustainability and simplicity, challenging the status quo, and investing in the right tools. By leveraging risk dashboards, businesses can strengthen their risk management framework, make more informed decisions, and ultimately enhance their overall resilience and performance.

c. Incident Reporting Systems
Incident reporting systems are a critical component of modern risk management practices in businesses. These systems enable the capture of hazards, near misses, and accidents, facilitating the identification of risks with severe consequences.

By effectively identifying, analyzing, and controlling risks through incident reporting, organizations can proactively prevent incidents and enhance safety.

Key benefits of incident reporting systems for risk management include:

i. Improved safety culture and trust:
A well-designed incident reporting system helps foster a 'safety first' culture, building psychological safety and trust among employees.

ii. Faster response to emergencies:
Incident reporting systems enable real-time reporting of incidents, allowing for swifter responses and mitigation of risks.

iii. Valuable data for analysis:
Incident reports provide data that can be analyzed to identify patterns, trends, and areas of concern, enabling informed decision-making and prioritization of risk management strategies.

iv. Improved compliance and risk mitigation:
A centralized incident reporting system helps organizations meet compliance requirements and be prepared for safety inspections.

To implement an effective incident reporting system, organizations should consider features such as mobile accessibility, automated workflows, notifications, and robust reporting capabilities.

By integrating incident reporting with broader Enterprise Risk Management systems, organizations can coordinate efforts across disciplines for maximum results.

In summary, incident reporting systems are essential for modern businesses to proactively identify hazards, analyze risks, and implement effective controls, ultimately enhancing safety and minimizing potential harm.

d. Continuous Monitoring and Auditing
Continuous monitoring and auditing systems are becoming increasingly important for modern risk management in business. These systems use automation and real-time data analysis to provide organizations with constant visibility into their risk, compliance, and control environments.
Some key benefits of continuous monitoring include:
   i. Analyzing 100% of data instead of just samples, removing subjectivity and the potential to miss suspicious activity
   ii. Uncovering deviations in real-time, enabling faster response and remediation
   iii. Improving the effectiveness of internal controls to minimize errors, misuse, abuse and fraud
   iv. Spreading compliance work throughout the year to potentially reduce costs
   v. Providing greater coverage to support a risk-based approach to compliance programs
   vi. Increasing productivity of compliance and audit teams by automating testing
   vii. Giving executives visibility into the organization's risk, security and compliance status

Implementing continuous monitoring involves defining the key controls to monitor, gathering transaction data, and developing automated tests to evaluate control compliance in near real-time.

This allows organizations to continuously assess their control environment and uncover issues before they escalate.

As business environments grow more complex, with data spread across systems and employees working remotely, continuous monitoring is becoming essential for effective risk management. It provides the real-time insight and automated oversight needed to navigate today's dynamic risk landscape.

e. Trend Analysis

Trend analysis is a crucial tool for modern risk management in business. By identifying patterns, changes, and opportunities in the business environment, trend analysis enables organizations to proactively manage risks and make informed decisions.

Some innovative ways to use trend analysis for risk management include:

i. Scenario planning:
Creating and analyzing multiple scenarios based on trends and uncertainties to identify risks, opportunities, and develop strategies to cope with them.

ii. Predictive analytics:
Employing advanced statistical models and machine learning algorithms to forecast future trends based on historical data and predict potential risks before they materialize.

iii. Sentiment analysis:
Monitoring social media, news, and other sources for shifts in public opinion to identify reputational risks and public relations challenges.

iv. Cross-industry benchmarking:
Conducting trend analysis across different sectors to identify emerging risks by comparing trends in related industries that may have downstream impacts.

v. Technology integration:
Integrating cutting-edge technologies, such as artificial intelligence (AI) and natural language processing (NLP), into trend analysis tools to automate the analysis of vast datasets and quickly identify and assess potential risks.

Real-time risk monitoring, enabled by predictive analytics and business intelligence tools, is crucial for empowering business resilience.

By continuously analyzing data from various sources, real-time risk monitoring creates a live stream of insights that decision-makers can tap into instantaneously, allowing them to detect anomalies and emerging risks before they escalate.

6 FINANCIAL RISK MANAGEMENT

Financial risk management is the practice of protecting a firm's economic value by identifying, measuring, and mitigating exposure to financial risks, primarily operational risk, credit risk, and market risk.

It is an essential element of a modern finance function that enables teams to develop strategies, policies and procedures to manage financial risks.

The key aspects of financial risk management include:
i. Identifying potential financial risks, such as defaults, fraud, legal challenges, fluctuations in interest rates or exchange rates, and price uncertainty along the supply chain.
ii. Assessing the likelihood and potential impact of identified risks.
iii. Developing and implementing strategies to mitigate or control the risks, such as holding insurance, diversifying investments, maintaining emergency funds, and generating multiple income streams.
iv. Continuously monitoring and adjusting risk management strategies as the business environment evolves.

Financial risk management is crucial for the long-term success of any organization. By understanding and addressing financial risks, companies can achieve their financial objectives, improve overall performance, and navigate the complex financial landscape.

In larger organizations, a dedicated risk manager or team may oversee enterprise risk management, but the finance team typically retains responsibility for tracking, quantifying and mitigating financial risks. Modern financial management systems enable finance teams to capture, integrate and analyze data from multiple sources to gain insights on risk probability, impact and mitigation.

a. Credit Risk

   Credit risk refers to the potential financial loss that a lender or creditor may incur when a borrower or counterparty fails to meet their contractual obligations, such as defaulting on loan repayments or failing to settle outstanding debts.

   Key Aspects of Credit Risk
   i. It arises from the possibility that a borrower may be unable or unwilling to repay their debt obligations, including principal and interest payments.
   ii. It is a significant concern for financial institutions, such as banks and credit unions, as well as non-financial businesses that extend credit to customers or engage in lending activities.
   iii. Effective credit risk management involves identifying, assessing, and mitigating the potential risks associated with extending credit to borrowers or counterparties.

   Assessing Credit Risk
   Lenders typically assess credit risk by evaluating the "Five Cs" of credit:
   i. Character:
      The borrower's creditworthiness, integrity, and willingness to repay the debt.
   ii. Capacity:
      The borrower's ability to generate sufficient income or cash flow to meet their debt obligations.
   iii. Capital:
      The borrower's financial resources, including assets, liabilities, and net worth.
   iv. Collateral:
      The assets or securities pledged by the borrower as a secondary source of repayment in case of default.
   v. Conditions:
      The economic and industry-specific factors that may impact the borrower's ability to repay the debt.

   Mitigating Credit Risk
   Businesses can mitigate credit risk through various strategies, including:

i. Implementing robust credit policies and procedures for evaluating borrowers' creditworthiness.
ii. Diversifying their credit portfolio across different industries, geographic regions, and borrower types.
iii. Utilizing credit risk models and scoring systems to assess and monitor credit risk exposure.
iv. Establishing credit limits and regularly reviewing and adjusting them based on changing circumstances.
v. Requiring collateral or guarantees from borrowers to secure the debt.
vi. Maintaining open communication with borrowers and monitoring their financial performance.
vii. Implementing early warning systems and contingency plans for potential defaults.

Importance of Credit Risk Management
Effective credit risk management is crucial for businesses to:
i. Protect their financial assets and maintain healthy cash flows.
ii. Minimize potential losses from defaults and bad debts.
iii. Ensure regulatory compliance and maintain a strong reputation in the market.
iv. Optimize lending practices and pricing strategies based on risk assessments.
v. Foster long-term financial stability and profitability.

In summary, credit risk is an inherent aspect of lending and extending credit, and its effective management is essential for businesses to safeguard their financial well-being and maintain a sustainable lending portfolio.

b. Market Risk
Market risk refers to the potential for losses arising from adverse movements in market factors such as interest rates, foreign exchange rates, equity and commodity prices, and their associated volatilities. It is a crucial risk that businesses, particularly financial institutions, must effectively manage to safeguard their financial stability and profitability.

Types of Market Risk
The main types of market risk include:

i. Interest Rate Risk:
The risk of losses due to changes in interest rates, which can impact the value of fixed-income securities, loans, and other interest-rate-sensitive instruments.
ii. Foreign Exchange Risk:
The risk of losses resulting from fluctuations in currency exchange rates, which can affect the value of assets, liabilities, and cash flows denominated in foreign currencies.
iii. Equity Risk:
The risk of losses due to changes in stock prices, which can impact the value of equity investments and equity-linked products.
iv. Commodity Risk:
The risk of losses caused by fluctuations in commodity prices, such as those of energy, agricultural products, and precious metals.

Measuring and Managing Market Risk
Financial institutions and businesses employ various techniques to measure and manage market risk, including:

i. Value-at-Risk (VaR):
A statistical measure that estimates the potential loss in value of a portfolio or position over a given time horizon and at a specific confidence level.
ii. Stress Testing:
A technique that evaluates the potential impact of extreme market scenarios on a portfolio or institution's financial position.
iii. Sensitivity Analysis:
An approach that measures the sensitivity of a portfolio or position to changes in specific market risk factors, such as interest rates or exchange rates.
iv. Hedging Strategies:
The use of derivative instruments, such as futures, options, and swaps, to offset or mitigate market risk exposures.
v. Diversification:
Spreading investments across different asset classes, sectors, and geographic regions to reduce the impact of market movements on the overall portfolio.

Importance of Market Risk Management

Effective market risk management is crucial for businesses, particularly financial institutions, for several reasons:

i. Financial Stability:
Proper management of market risk helps protect businesses from significant losses and ensures their financial stability, even during periods of market volatility.

ii. Regulatory Compliance:
Financial institutions are subject to strict regulatory requirements regarding market risk management, such as the Basel Accords and the Fundamental Review of the Trading Book (FRTB) framework.

iii. Competitive Advantage:
Robust market risk management practices can provide businesses with a competitive edge by enabling them to make informed decisions and capitalize on market opportunities while managing risks effectively.

iv. Investor Confidence:
Strong market risk management practices can enhance investor confidence in a business, as it demonstrates a commitment to prudent risk management and financial stability.

In today's dynamic and interconnected global markets, effective market risk management is essential for businesses to navigate uncertainties, seize opportunities, and maintain long-term financial resilience.

c. Liquidity Risk

Liquidity risk refers to the potential inability of a business or financial institution to meet its short-term financial obligations due to a lack of readily available cash or liquid assets. It arises when there is a mismatch between the entity's assets and liabilities, making it challenging to convert assets into cash without incurring substantial losses.

Key Points about Liquidity Risk are

i. Inability to Meet Obligations:
Liquidity risk manifests when an entity faces difficulty in fulfilling its immediate financial commitments, such as paying creditors, suppliers, employees, or meeting debt repayments.

ii. Mismatch of Assets and Liabilities:
The root cause of liquidity risk is an imbalance between an entity's liquid assets and its short-term liabilities. If assets cannot be easily converted into cash, the entity may struggle to meet its obligations.

iii. Cash Flow Disruptions:
Poor cash flow management, unexpected expenses, or a sudden increase in liabilities can exacerbate liquidity risk, leading to a shortage of available funds.

iv. Market Liquidity Risk:
This type of liquidity risk arises when an entity is unable to execute transactions at prevailing market prices due to inadequate market depth or disruptions, making it difficult to sell assets quickly.

v. Funding Liquidity Risk:
This risk pertains to the challenges an entity may face in obtaining the necessary funds or financing to meet its short-term financial obligations.

Consequences of Liquidity Risk
Unmanaged liquidity risk can have severe consequences for businesses, including:

i. Financial losses and operational disruptions
ii. Inability to meet payroll or pay suppliers/creditors
iii. Reputational damage and loss of investor/customer confidence
iv. Forced asset sales at unfavorable prices
v. Increased borrowing costs or difficulty obtaining financing
vi. In extreme cases, insolvency or bankruptcy

Liquidity Risk Management Strategies
Effective liquidity risk management involves implementing proactive strategies, such as:

i. Maintaining a balanced portfolio of liquid assets
ii. Diversifying funding sources (e.g., bank loans, credit lines, financial instruments)
iii. Optimizing asset and liability maturities to avoid imbalances
iv. Continuous monitoring of cash flows and market conditions
v. Establishing liquidity reserves or emergency funds

vi. Accurate cash flow forecasting and budgeting
vii. Analyzing counterparty and external risks (e.g., market volatility, economic crises)

By implementing these strategies, businesses can mitigate liquidity risk, ensure financial stability, and maintain the ability to meet their obligations in a timely manner, even during periods of financial stress or unforeseen events.

d. Operational Risk

Operational risk refers to the potential losses or disruptions that can arise from inadequate or failed internal processes, systems, human errors, or external events affecting an organization's operations and business continuity.

It encompasses a wide range of risks that businesses face in their day-to-day operations and can have significant financial, reputational, and regulatory consequences if not managed effectively.

Key Aspects of Operational Risk are
i. Internal Processes:
Flaws or inefficiencies in internal processes, such as inadequate controls, poor documentation, or lack of standardization, can lead to operational failures and losses.
ii. People:
Human errors, misconduct, inadequate training, or staffing issues can contribute to operational risks. For example, the Equifax data breach in 2017 was caused by a failure to patch a known vulnerability due to human error.
iii. Systems:
Technological failures, cybersecurity threats, system outages, or inadequate system capacity can disrupt operations and expose businesses to operational risks. The WannaCry ransomware attack in 2017 highlighted the vulnerability of systems to cyber threats.
iv. External Events:
Natural disasters, political instability, regulatory changes, or third-party failures can impact business operations and pose operational risks. The 2011 Fukushima nuclear disaster

disrupted global supply chains, demonstrating the impact of external events.

Importance of Operational Risk Management (ORM)
Effective ORM is crucial for businesses to ensure business continuity, minimize losses, maintain compliance, and protect their reputation.

It involves proactively identifying, assessing, mitigating, and monitoring operational risks through robust processes, controls, and strategies.

i. Business Continuity:
By anticipating and mitigating operational risks, businesses can maintain uninterrupted operations or minimize disruptions, ensuring continuity of critical processes and services.

ii. Loss Prevention:
Operational failures can result in significant financial losses, legal liabilities, and reputational damage. ORM helps prevent or reduce the impact of such losses.

iii. Compliance:
Many industries have regulatory requirements related to operational risk management. Effective ORM ensures compliance with these regulations and avoids penalties or sanctions.

iv. Reputation Protection:
Operational incidents, such as data breaches or service disruptions, can severely damage a company's reputation. ORM helps safeguard a business's brand and stakeholder trust.

v. Strategic Alignment:
By identifying and addressing operational risks, businesses can align their strategies and operations more effectively, enabling them to seize opportunities while managing risks proactively.

In today's complex business environment, where operational risks are diverse and constantly evolving, robust ORM practices are essential for businesses to maintain resilience, agility, and a competitive edge.

e. Hedging and Derivatives
Hedging and derivatives are crucial tools for modern risk management in businesses. Here's an explanation of these concepts:

Hedging
Hedging is a risk management strategy that involves taking an offsetting position in a derivative to reduce the risk of adverse price movements in an asset or portfolio. It aims to protect against potential losses by counterbalancing exposures to variables like interest rates, commodity prices, or currency exchange rates.
For example, an airline company might use crude oil futures contracts to hedge against rising fuel costs. If oil prices increase, the gains from the futures contracts would offset the higher fuel expenses, protecting the airline's profitability.

Businesses can use various hedging strategies with derivatives, such as:
i. Short hedging:
Selling a derivative to protect against a potential price decrease in an owned asset.
ii. Long hedging:
Buying a derivative to protect against a potential price increase in an asset that needs to be purchased.
iii. Portfolio hedging:
Using derivatives to hedge the overall risk of a portfolio containing multiple assets.
iv. Cross hedging:
Hedging an asset with a derivative based on a different but correlated asset when a direct hedge is unavailable or too costly.

Derivatives
Derivatives are financial instruments that derive their value from an underlying asset, such as stocks, bonds, commodities, currencies, interest rates, or market indexes. Common examples of derivatives include:
i. Futures contracts:
Agreements to buy or sell an asset at a predetermined price and date in the future.

ii. Options contracts:
   Give the holder the right, but not the obligation, to buy (call option) or sell (put option) an underlying asset at a predetermined price within a specific timeframe.
iii. Swaps:
   Contracts where two parties exchange cash flows based on a notional principal amount, such as interest rate swaps or currency swaps.
iv. Forwards:
   Customized contracts between two parties to buy or sell an asset at a specified price on a future date.

Derivatives allow businesses to transfer risk from one party to another. They enable hedging against unfavorable price movements, locking in prices, or speculating on asset prices.

Importance of Hedging and Derivatives in Risk Management
i. Hedging with derivatives is crucial for modern businesses as it helps:
ii. Mitigate risks associated with price fluctuations, interest rates, and currency exchange rates.
iii. Reduce volatility and stabilize cash flows, making financial planning more predictable.
iv. Transfer risks to parties more willing or able to bear them.
v. Comply with regulatory requirements or internal risk management policies.
vi. Enhance profitability by locking in favorable prices or rates.

However, it's important to note that hedging does not eliminate risk entirely but rather aims to manage and mitigate it. Effective risk management strategies often involve a combination of hedging with derivatives and other risk management techniques.

7 ENTERPRISE RISK MANAGEMENT (ERM)

Enterprise Risk Management (ERM) is a comprehensive and integrated approach to managing risks across an entire organization. It involves identifying, assessing, prioritizing, and mitigating risks that could potentially impact the achievement of an organization's strategic objectives, operations, and financial performance.

Introduction to Enterprise Risk Management
In today's dynamic and uncertain business environment, organizations face a multitude of risks, ranging from strategic, operational, financial, legal, and reputational risks. These risks can originate from both internal and external sources, and their impact can be far-reaching and interconnected.

Traditional risk management practices, which often focus on specific departments or functions, may fail to capture the interconnectedness of risks and their potential cascading effects across the organization.

ERM addresses this challenge by adopting a holistic and integrated approach to risk management. It recognizes that risks do not exist in isolation and that their impact can transcend departmental boundaries. By considering risks from an enterprise-wide perspective, ERM enables organizations to identify, assess, and manage risks in a coordinated and consistent manner, aligning risk management strategies with the organization's overall objectives and risk appetite.

Key Components of Enterprise Risk Management
The successful implementation of ERM involves several key components:
i. Risk Identification:
    Identifying potential risks that could impact the organization's ability to achieve its objectives. This includes risks related to strategy, operations, compliance, financial performance, and reputation.

ii. Risk Assessment:
Analyzing and evaluating the likelihood and potential impact of identified risks, both individually and in combination with other risks.
iii. Risk Prioritization:
Prioritizing risks based on their potential impact and likelihood, allowing organizations to focus their resources on the most critical risks.
iv. Risk Mitigation:
Developing and implementing strategies to mitigate or manage identified risks, such as risk avoidance, risk reduction, risk transfer, or risk acceptance.
v. Risk Monitoring and Reporting:
Continuously monitoring and reporting on the effectiveness of risk management strategies, as well as identifying emerging risks and changes in the risk landscape.
vi. Risk Governance and Culture:
Establishing a strong risk governance framework, including clear roles and responsibilities, and fostering a risk-aware culture throughout the organization.

By implementing an effective ERM program, organizations can better anticipate and respond to potential risks, make more informed decisions, and ultimately enhance their resilience and long-term sustainability.

a. ERM Frameworks

Enterprise Risk Management (ERM) frameworks provide a structured approach to identifying, assessing, and managing risks across an organization in a comprehensive and integrated manner.

Here's an overview of modern ERM frameworks and their key aspects:

i. COSO ERM Framework
The Committee of Sponsoring Organizations of the Treadway Commission (COSO) ERM framework is one of the most widely adopted ERM frameworks globally.
It consists of the following key components:

1. Governance and Culture:
   Establishing the appropriate tone at the top, ethical values, oversight responsibilities, and a risk-aware culture.
2. Strategy and Objective-Setting:
   Ensuring that risk management is aligned with the organization's strategy and business objectives.
3. Performance:
   Identifying and assessing risks that may impact the achievement of strategic and operational objectives.
4. Review and Revision:
   Monitoring and revising the ERM components to adapt to changing business contexts.
5. Information, Communication, and Reporting:
   Ensuring effective communication and reporting of risk information across the organization.

The COSO ERM framework emphasizes integrating risk management into strategic planning, decision-making, and day-to-day operations.

ii. ISO 31000 Risk Management Standard
The ISO 31000 is an international standard that provides principles, framework, and processes for effective risk management. Key aspects include:
1. Principles:
2. Establishing the foundations and commitments for managing risk effectively.
3. Framework:
4. Integrating risk management into the organization's governance, strategy, and operations.
5. Process:
6. A systematic approach to identifying, analyzing, evaluating, treating, monitoring, and reviewing risks.

The ISO 31000 standard emphasizes continual improvement, stakeholder engagement, and creating value through risk management

iii. RIMS Risk Maturity Model

The Risk and Insurance Management Society (RIMS) Risk Maturity Model provides a roadmap for organizations to assess and improve their risk management capabilities.

It consists of the following maturity levels:

1. Ad Hoc:
   Unstructured and reactive risk management approach.
2. Fragmented:
   Siloed risk management efforts within business units.
3. Integrated:
   Coordinated risk management across the organization.
4. Advanced:
   Risk management is embedded in strategic decision-making.
5. Leadership:
   Risk management is a competitive advantage and a core capability.

The RIMS model helps organizations benchmark their risk management maturity and develop a roadmap for continuous improvement.

Key Aspects of Modern ERM Frameworks are

1. Integration:
   Embedding risk management into strategic planning, decision-making, and operational processes across the organization.
2. Governance and Culture:
   Establishing a risk-aware culture, clear roles and responsibilities, and effective oversight mechanisms.

3. Stakeholder Engagement:
   Involving stakeholders in the risk management process and ensuring effective communication and reporting.
4. Continual Improvement:
   Regularly monitoring, reviewing, and adapting the ERM framework to changing business contexts and emerging risks.
5. Technology and Data:
   Leveraging technology, data analytics, and automation to enhance risk identification, assessment, and monitoring capabilities.

Modern ERM frameworks emphasize a holistic and integrated approach to risk management, aligning it with the organization's strategic objectives and embedding it into decision-making processes. They also highlight the importance of a risk-aware culture, stakeholder engagement, and continual improvement through monitoring and adaptation.

b. Integrating ERM into Business Strategy
   Integrating Enterprise Risk Management (ERM) into business strategy is crucial for modern risk management in organizations. Here are the key points:
   i. Aligning Risk Management with Strategic Objectives
      Effective ERM aligns risk management practices with the organization's strategic objectives and decision-making processes. This ensures that potential risks are identified, assessed, and managed in the context of the organization's overall goals and strategies. By integrating ERM into strategic planning, organizations can make informed decisions and adopt strategies that optimize risk-taking while pursuing growth opportunities.
   ii. Comprehensive Risk Identification and Assessment
       ERM provides a structured and comprehensive approach to

identifying and assessing risks across the entire organization, including strategic, operational, financial, and compliance risks. This holistic view enables organizations to understand their overall risk exposure and prioritize risk management efforts accordingly.

iii. Improved Decision-Making and Resource Allocation

By integrating ERM into strategic planning, organizations can make more informed decisions about resource allocation, capital investments, and risk mitigation strategies. This helps ensure that resources are directed towards the most critical risks and opportunities, enhancing the organization's resilience and competitiveness.

iv. Enhanced Stakeholder Confidence and Transparency

Effective ERM demonstrates to stakeholders, such as investors, regulators, and customers, that the organization has a robust risk management framework in place. This can increase stakeholder confidence, improve corporate reputation, and enhance transparency, which is increasingly important in today's business environment.

v. Continuous Monitoring and Adaptation

ERM is an ongoing process that involves continuously monitoring and adapting to changes in the risk landscape. By integrating ERM into business strategy, organizations can proactively identify emerging risks and opportunities, enabling them to respond swiftly and effectively to changing market conditions and business environments.

In summary, integrating ERM into business strategy is essential for modern risk management. It aligns risk management practices with strategic objectives, provides a comprehensive view of risks, improves decision-making and resource allocation, enhances stakeholder confidence, and enables continuous monitoring and adaptation to changing risk landscapes.

c. Governance and Leadership in ERM
   Governance and leadership play a crucial role in effective Enterprise Risk Management (ERM) for modern risk management in businesses.

   Here are some key points:
   Governance in ERM
   i. The board of directors and senior management are responsible for setting the tone and establishing an appropriate risk culture within the organization.
   ii. A strong governance structure with clear roles, responsibilities, and accountability for risk management is essential. This includes defining risk appetite, risk tolerance levels, and risk management policies and procedures.
   iii. Effective governance ensures that risk management is integrated into strategic planning, decision-making processes, and day-to-day operations across the organization.
   iv. Governance frameworks, such as the COSO ERM framework, provide guidance on establishing an effective risk governance structure, including oversight roles for the board and executive management.

   Leadership in ERM
   i. Risk leadership involves envisioning and promoting a risk-aware culture, fostering critical thinking about risks, and driving the implementation of ERM across the organization.
   ii. Effective risk leaders have a holistic view of the organization's risk landscape and can navigate the complexities of risk interactions and interdependencies.
   iii. Risk leaders should champion ERM as a strategic tool, ensuring that risk insights inform strategic planning and decision-making processes.
   iv. Risk leadership involves continuous communication and collaboration with stakeholders, promoting transparency and accountability in risk management practices.

v. Risk leaders should foster an environment that encourages open dialogue, challenge assumptions, and consider alternative perspectives when assessing and responding to risks.

By establishing robust governance structures and promoting effective risk leadership, organizations can enhance their ERM readiness, enabling them to proactively identify, assess, and mitigate risks, ultimately supporting sustainable organizational resilience and strategic success.

d. Building a Risk-Aware Culture
Building a risk-aware culture is essential for effective enterprise risk management (ERM) in modern businesses. A strong risk culture aligns corporate values, beliefs, and attitudes with proactive risk management practices across all levels of the organization.
Key strategies for developing a risk-aware culture include:
i. Starting from the Top Down
Executive leadership must prioritize risk culture, communicate its importance, and lead by example. C-suite and board members should demonstrate desired risk-related behaviors and decisions to drive cultural change.
ii. Embedding Risk Awareness in Training
Onboarding and ongoing training should integrate risk management concepts and vocabulary. Customized training based on roles and business units helps employees understand individual risk responsibilities.
iii. Increasing Risk Visibility
Providing employees visibility into risks enables them to understand actions needed to manage them. Seeking employee feedback strengthens risk culture by leveraging their knowledge and insights.
iv. Aligning Incentives with Risk Performance
Embedding risk metrics into compensation and reward systems reinforces positive risk-related behaviors.

Accountability for actions that harm risk management is also important.
v. Communicating Risk in Business Terms
Risk concepts and practices should be conveyed in simple, pragmatic language that resonates with employees. Using terms they understand helps them grasp how risk applies to their day-to-day roles.
vi. Integrating Risk into Decision-Making
Incorporating risk considerations into strategic planning and operational decisions enables better-informed choices. This lays the foundation for a systematic, collaborative approach to risk management.

By implementing these strategies, organizations can cultivate a risk-aware culture that improves agility, employee engagement, resource allocation, and compliance adherence. Embracing risk management as a shared responsibility empowers every employee to contribute to the company's long-term resilience and success.

e. Risk Appetite and Tolerance
Risk appetite and risk tolerance are two key concepts in enterprise risk management (ERM) that help organizations define their approach to managing risks.

Risk Appetite:
Risk appetite is the amount and type of risk an organization is willing to pursue or retain in order to achieve its strategic objectives. It reflects the organization's willingness to take on risk and is influenced by factors such as the organization's values, culture, and management philosophy. A well-defined risk appetite helps an organization make informed decisions about the risks it is willing to accept and those it wants to avoid or mitigate.

Risk Tolerance:
Risk tolerance refers to the acceptable variation in outcomes related to specific performance measures tied to objectives.

It establishes the boundaries of acceptable risk taking and helps an organization determine if a risk is within acceptable limits.

Risk tolerance levels are typically more specific and measurable than risk appetite. For example, an organization may have a risk tolerance of no more than a 5% decrease in revenue or a 10% increase in operating costs.

In modern risk management, risk appetite and tolerance are used to align an organization's risk management practices with its strategic objectives.

By defining their risk appetite and tolerance, organizations can:
i. Make informed decisions about the risks they are willing to take on in pursuit of their goals
ii. Prioritize and allocate resources to manage the most critical risks
iii. Establish clear boundaries for risk-taking and ensure that risks are within acceptable limits
iv. Communicate their risk management approach to stakeholders, such as investors and regulators

Effective ERM requires organizations to regularly review and update their risk appetite and tolerance to adapt to changing business conditions and emerging risks. By incorporating risk appetite and tolerance into their decision-making processes, organizations can take a more strategic and proactive approach to managing risks, enabling them to seize opportunities and build resilience in today's dynamic business environment.

8 REGULATORY AND COMPLIANCE RISK

Regulatory and compliance risk refers to the potential for legal or financial penalties, material financial loss, or damage to an organization's reputation resulting from its failure to comply with laws, regulations, rules, related self-regulatory organization standards, and codes of conduct applicable to its activities.

In today's complex business environment, organizations face an ever-increasing array of regulatory requirements across various domains such as data privacy, financial reporting, anti-corruption, and environmental protection. Failure to adhere to these regulations can expose companies to significant risks, including hefty fines, lawsuits, and reputational damage that can undermine stakeholder trust and impact financial performance.

Effective regulatory and compliance risk management is crucial for modern businesses to navigate this challenging landscape successfully. By proactively identifying, assessing, and mitigating compliance risks, organizations can protect themselves from potential pitfalls, maintain a positive reputation, and focus on achieving their strategic objectives.

a. Understanding Regulatory Requirements
Effective risk management in today's business environment requires a comprehensive understanding of the evolving regulatory landscape. Regulations play a crucial role in shaping how organizations identify, assess, and mitigate risks. Here are key aspects to consider:

  i. Compliance is a Critical Component of Risk Management
  While compliance and risk management are distinct, they are closely interrelated. Compliance focuses on adhering to laws,

regulations, and industry standards, while risk management encompasses a broader range of potential risks, including operational, financial, strategic, and reputational. However, compliance risk is a key component of overall risk management.

ii. Regulations Intentionally Expose Organizations to Non-Compliance Risk

Many regulations, such as capital adequacy rules, health and safety regulations, and environmental protection regimes, purposefully expose organizations to the risk of non-compliance. This is because regulations seek to manage risks faced by stakeholders, including employees, customers, and communities. Effective risk management requires organizations to proactively address compliance risks.

iii. Compliance is a Creative Process Involving Negotiation and Interaction

Determining compliance is not always straightforward, as regulatory laws often involve broad standards and delegate discretion to officials. Compliance requires assessing the risks associated with activities and their acceptability. This process involves negotiation and interaction between regulatory agencies and regulated entities.

iv. Regulatory Requirements are Evolving Rapidly

The risk and regulatory landscape are rapidly changing, with new rules and requirements emerging frequently. Organizations must have a flexible and responsive infrastructure to adapt to these changes. This includes having a governing body that closely monitors regulatory developments, assesses potential implications, and communicates critical details throughout the organization.

v. Effective Risk Management Requires a Comprehensive and Transparent Approach

To navigate modern regulatory requirements, organizations should adopt a comprehensive and transparent approach to risk management. This involves sharing regulatory knowledge throughout the entire organization with full transparency, from the top down. Employees should have access to the information needed to identify and mitigate potential risks.

vi. Leveraging Data and Systems is Key to Proactive Risk Management

A data-centric approach, powered by modern systems, is crucial for being proactive in an ever-shifting risk and regulatory landscape. Quality data can help organizations monitor regulatory changes in real-time, while advanced analytics can predict potential risks and assess the effectiveness of risk management strategies. Embracing digital tools and technologies is essential for navigating today's complex risk environment.

In summary, understanding and adhering to regulatory requirements is a critical component of modern risk management. Organizations must adopt a proactive, comprehensive, and data-driven approach to identify, assess, and mitigate compliance risks while remaining agile in the face of a rapidly evolving regulatory landscape.

b. Compliance Programs

Compliance programs are essential for modern businesses to effectively manage risks and ensure adherence to relevant laws, regulations, and industry standards. As the regulatory landscape continues to evolve and new risks emerge, organizations must adopt a proactive and integrated approach to compliance and risk management.

Importance of Compliance Programs
Compliance programs help organizations:

i. Avoid legal penalties and fines for non-compliance, which can be substantial and damaging to the business.
ii. Protect their reputation and maintain stakeholder trust by demonstrating a commitment to ethical and responsible

business practices.
iii. Identify and mitigate potential risks that could threaten the organization's objectives, such as cybersecurity threats, operational failures, and financial risks.
iv. Stay informed about changes in regulations and adapt their policies and procedures accordingly to maintain compliance.

Key Components of Effective Compliance Programs
i. Risk assessment: Identify and prioritize compliance risks based on their likelihood and potential impact on the organization.
ii. Policies and procedures: Develop clear and comprehensive policies and procedures to guide employee behavior and ensure compliance with relevant laws and regulations.
iii. Training and communication: Provide regular training to employees on compliance requirements and expectations, and establish open communication channels for reporting potential issues.
iv. Monitoring and testing: Regularly monitor compliance controls and test their effectiveness to identify areas for improvement and ensure ongoing compliance.
v. Incident response and remediation: Establish a process for responding to and remediating compliance incidents, including root cause analysis and implementation of corrective actions.

Integrating Compliance and Risk Management
To maximize the effectiveness of compliance programs, organizations should integrate them with their overall risk management strategy. This involves:
i. Aligning compliance and risk management objectives:
Ensure that compliance and risk management efforts are working towards the same goals and supporting the organization's overall business strategy.
ii. Sharing risk information:
Establish processes for sharing risk information between

compliance, risk management, and other relevant functions to enable a holistic view of the organization's risk profile.
iii. Coordinating compliance and risk assessments:
Conduct joint compliance and risk assessments to identify and prioritize risks, and develop integrated mitigation strategies.
iv. Leveraging technology:
Utilize compliance and risk management software to centralize data, automate processes, and enable real-time monitoring and reporting.

By adopting a modern, integrated approach to compliance and risk management, organizations can enhance their resilience, protect their assets, and position themselves for long-term success in an increasingly complex business environment.

c. Internal Audits

Internal audits play a crucial role in modern risk management for businesses. By assessing and evaluating an organization's internal controls, governance processes, and risk management practices, internal audits help identify potential risks and ensure the company is operating effectively and efficiently.

There are several key aspects to effective internal auditing for risk management:

i. Risk-Based Approach
A risk-based internal auditing approach focuses on identifying, assessing, and prioritizing the most significant risks facing the organization. This involves:
1. Establishing risk criteria and identifying key risks relevant to the company's objectives
2. Allocating audit resources based on the identified risks
3. Developing a risk-based audit plan that addresses management's highest priority risks

By aligning audits with the organization's risk profile and risk tolerance, this approach ensures audits provide the most value in managing critical risks.

ii. Continuous Monitoring

Continuous auditing involves real-time or near real-time monitoring of key risk indicators using technology and automated tools. This allows internal auditors to regularly assess and report on emerging risks, enabling swift responses. Continuous monitoring is a proactive approach to risk management compared to traditional periodic audits.

iii. Engaging the Business

Effective internal audit management requires frequent communication and engagement with the business units being audited. This helps build bridges between internal audit and the organization, ensuring everyone understands the audit objectives and feels part of the process. Explaining the audit benefits, such as increased efficiency and better processes, helps gain buy-in.

iv. Identifying Key Controls

A critical part of the internal audit process is identifying the key controls that manage significant risks. This involves pinpointing the most important controls through a risk assessment, and then testing the design and operating effectiveness of those controls. Capturing findings in writing builds a compliant audit trail.

v. Reporting and Follow-Up

Proactive reporting is essential, with the audit report being an integral part of the fieldwork process. Auditors should not wait until the end to start writing the report, as findings may be forgotten. Reporting should be timely and include agreed-upon actions to remediate any control deficiencies identified.

By adopting these risk-based internal auditing approaches, organizations can move beyond mere compliance to actively enhance their decision-making processes and overall resilience.

This helps internal audit be recognized as a trusted advisor that adds value to the business

d. Anti-Money Laundering (AML)
Anti-Money Laundering (AML) is a critical component of modern risk management for businesses, particularly in the financial services industry. The current AML landscape requires a proactive and adaptive approach, underpinned by robust regulatory compliance, advanced technological solutions, and constant vigilance against emerging threats.

Traditional AML tactics, such as rule-based systems and manual investigations, are becoming insufficient due to several factors:
i. The complexity and scale of financial transactions have grown exponentially with globalization and digitalization, making it difficult for traditional AML systems to effectively monitor and analyze the vast amounts of data generated.
ii. Money launderers have become more sophisticated, employing new technologies and methods to evade detection, exploiting the gaps and weaknesses in traditional AML systems.
iii. Traditional AML systems often generate a high number of false positives, leading to inefficiencies and increased operational costs.
iv. Regulatory expectations and requirements for AML compliance have become more stringent, requiring financial institutions to adopt a risk-based approach that is beyond the capabilities of many traditional AML systems.

To combat these challenges, businesses are increasingly turning to advanced technologies such as AI and machine learning, big data analytics, and cloud computing. These tools can significantly improve detection accuracy, streamline compliance processes, reduce costs, and enable proactive risk management, making them a crucial part of modern AML efforts.

A robust AML compliance program also requires a comprehensive risk assessment to identify and mitigate potential risks. This process involves understanding the conditions that increase the chances of a customer's involvement in money laundering or terrorist financing, known as Key Risk Indicators (KRI). By adopting a risk-based approach, businesses can ensure more effective detection and mitigation of potential risks.

Moreover, implementing AML practices can enhance operational efficiency for businesses of all sizes. By utilizing the right solutions, businesses can effectively address challenges, identify areas of high risk, and efficiently manage gaps or weaknesses. This approach leads to significant cost savings and improves overall performance by providing evidence-based support for business decisions.

In conclusion, AML is a critical component of modern risk management for businesses, particularly in the financial services industry. By adopting a proactive and adaptive approach, leveraging advanced technologies, and implementing comprehensive risk assessments, businesses can effectively combat money laundering and other financial crimes while enhancing operational efficiency and regulatory compliance

e. Data Protection and Privacy Regulations
Data protection and privacy regulations have become increasingly important for modern businesses to manage risks effectively.

Here are the key points to understand:
i. The Role of Risk Management in Data Protection
Risk management is a critical tool for ensuring that data is processed appropriately and that risks to individual privacy are mitigated. The goal is not to eliminate all risk, but to reduce it as much as practical and be explicit about the remaining risks. Risk assessments help determine when notification or other

actions are necessary, and ensure that restrictions on data processing are proportionate to the risks presented.

ii. Privacy Risk Assessments

A privacy risk assessment is used to identify, assess, and mitigate possible risks to people's and companies' data. It helps organizations understand their data collection, usage, and sharing policies and the associated privacy risks. Common names include Privacy Impact Assessment (PIA) or Data Protection Impact Assessment (DPIA).

iii. Why Businesses Need Privacy Risk Assessments
1. Compliance with privacy regulations like GDPR, CCPA, PIPEDA which require personal data management and control
2. Meeting customer expectations for data protection and building trust
3. Identifying and mitigating internal security risks to avoid data breaches and their consequences

iv. Benefits of Privacy Risk Assessments
1. Preparing for compliance audits and customer requests
2. Making informed decisions about data processing activities
3. Demonstrating accountability and transparency
4. Identifying and mitigating risks before they occur

v. Best Practices for Implementing Privacy Controls
1. Lead with Privacy by Design - embed data protection principles into system design and processes
2. Conduct a Privacy Risk Assessment - identify potential threats and vulnerabilities
3. Implement Strong Access Controls - limit access to sensitive data
4. Encrypt Sensitive Data - protect data at rest and in transit
5. Educate Employees - train on data security best practices
6. Develop Incident Response Plans - establish procedures for responding to breaches

vi. Key Elements of Data Protection Regulations
   1. Lawful processing - data must be obtained legally, usually through consent, for a specific purpose
   2. Purpose limitation - data cannot be used for unauthorized surveillance or unconnected purposes without consent
   3. User rights - rights to obtain, correct, and see how data is being used
   4. Independent oversight - processing must be monitored by an appropriate authority
   5. Privacy-enhancing technologies - use of technologies like tokenization to protect privacy

In summary, data protection and privacy regulations require businesses to proactively manage risks through privacy assessments, strong access controls, encryption, employee training, and incident response plans. Implementing these best practices helps ensure compliance, build customer trust, and avoid the costly consequences of data breaches.

9 TECHNOLOGY AND CYBER RISK

In the modern era, businesses are increasingly reliant on technology to drive innovation, efficiency, and growth. However, this heavy reliance on digital systems also exposes organizations to a myriad of cyber risks that can have severe consequences, from financial losses to reputational damage and legal liabilities. Cyber risk management has emerged as a critical discipline to help organizations navigate these evolving threats and protect their digital assets.

Cyber risk management is the proactive process of identifying, assessing, and mitigating the risks that emanate from the digital world. It involves a structured approach to ensure organizations can effectively identify, assess, prioritize, and respond to cyber risks. By implementing robust cyber risk management practices, businesses can safeguard their data, operations, and reputation in the face of ever-evolving cyber threats.

Understanding Cyber Risks
To manage cyber risks effectively, it's essential to understand the key components:
  i. Threats:
     These can arise from various sources, such as cybercriminals, nation-states, hacktivists, and even insiders.
  ii. Vulnerabilities:
     Weaknesses in systems, processes, or human behavior that can be exploited by threats.
  iii. Likelihood:
     The probability of a threat exploiting a vulnerability.
  iv. Impact:
     The potential consequences of a successful cyber-attack, which can be financial, operational, reputational, or regulatory

In today's hyper-connected world, where technology is the backbone of business operations, cyber risk management has become a critical discipline for organizations of all sizes. By understanding the key components of cyber risks, implementing a structured risk management process, and leveraging the expertise of cybersecurity risk managers, businesses can build resilient digital environments that foster innovation and growth while mitigating the risks posed by evolving cyber threats.

a. Cybersecurity Threats and Vulnerabilities

Cybersecurity threats and vulnerabilities are a major concern for modern businesses as they navigate the complex landscape of risk management. Some of the key threats and vulnerabilities that organizations face today include:

i. Evolving Threat Landscape

The cybersecurity threat landscape is constantly evolving, with new threats emerging regularly. In 2022, there were over 25,000 new common IT security vulnerabilities and exposures (CVEs) reported, the highest annual figure ever. Cybersecurity risk managers must stay informed about the latest threats and prioritize vulnerabilities based on their severity and potential impact on the organization.

ii. Expanded Attack Surface

The proliferation of remote work, cloud-based technologies, and Internet-of-Things (IoT) devices has expanded the attack surface for organizations. Managing this extended security perimeter presents challenges in ensuring consistent security measures, monitoring, and safeguarding sensitive data across various environments. Cybersecurity risk managers must implement robust security controls, including network segmentation, endpoint security solutions, virtual private networks, multi-factor authentication, and cloud security measures.

iii. Cross-Domain Risks

The security perimeter now extends far beyond IT, with convergence between IT, operational technology (OT), and IoT creating complex cross-domain security challenges due to different technologies, protocols, and cybersecurity requirements. Cybersecurity risk managers must develop comprehensive security policies and frameworks that encompass all domains, ensuring a unified approach to cybersecurity.

iv. Third-Party and Supply Chain Risks
Organizations are increasingly reliant on third-party vendors and partners, which introduces additional risks. A Ponemon Institute study estimates the average company shares confidential information with 583 third parties. Cybersecurity risk managers must evaluate and manage the risks associated with third-party vendors and ensure they adhere to security standards and guidelines.

v. Insider Threats
Insider threats, such as disgruntled employees or contractors, can pose significant risks to an organization's security. Cybersecurity risk managers must implement access controls, monitor user activity, and provide cybersecurity training to employees to mitigate insider threats.

To manage these threats and vulnerabilities, organizations must adopt a comprehensive cybersecurity risk management approach that includes:
1. Developing a cybersecurity risk management strategy tailored to the organization's unique needs
2. Maintaining an inventory of organizational assets and understanding their associated vulnerabilities
3. Identifying and assessing cybersecurity threats and vulnerabilities through rigorous analysis
4. Proposing and implementing appropriate risk treatment options, such as security controls and mitigation strategies
5. Continuously monitoring and ensuring the effectiveness of implemented controls
6. Engaging senior management and the Board of Directors in cybersecurity risk management

7. Leveraging automated solutions for real-time risk assessment and mitigation
8. Regularly testing security controls through penetration testing, vulnerability assessments, and tabletop exercises

By adopting a proactive and holistic approach to cybersecurity risk management, organizations can better protect themselves against evolving threats and vulnerabilities in the modern business landscape.

b. Data Breach Response

Data breaches are a serious threat to modern businesses, with the potential to cause significant financial losses, reputational damage, and regulatory penalties. In today's digital landscape, where data is the lifeblood of organizations, a well-structured data breach response plan is crucial for effective risk management.

Key Steps in Data Breach Response

i. Containment:
The first step is to contain the breach and limit its impact. This involves identifying the source of the breach, isolating affected systems, and preventing further data loss or unauthorized access.

ii. Assessment:
Once the breach is contained, it's essential to assess the damage. This includes determining what type of data was affected, how much data was compromised, and which individuals or entities were impacted.

iii. Notification:
Depending on the nature and severity of the breach, organizations may be required to notify affected individuals, regulatory authorities, and other stakeholders. Timely and transparent communication is crucial to maintain trust and mitigate reputational damage.

iv. Investigation:
A thorough investigation should be conducted to determine the root cause of the breach, identify any vulnerabilities in the system, and gather evidence for potential legal action or regulatory compliance.

v. Remediation and Evaluation:
Based on the findings of the investigation, organizations should implement remedial measures to address the vulnerabilities and prevent similar breaches in the future. This may involve updating security protocols, providing employee training, or implementing new technologies.

Best Practices for Data Breach Response

i. Develop an Incident Response Plan:
Establish a comprehensive incident response plan that outlines the roles, responsibilities, and procedures to be followed in the event of a data breach.

ii. Conduct Regular Risk Assessments:
Regularly assess the risks to your organization's data, including potential threats, vulnerabilities, and the potential impact of a breach.

iii. Implement Strong Security Controls:
Utilize robust security measures such as multi-factor authentication, strong password requirements, and regular patch management to reduce the risk of data breaches.

iv. Maintain Comprehensive Data Backups:
Ensure that critical data is regularly backed up using the 3-2-1 backup methodology (three copies of data, on two different forms of media, with one copy stored off-site).

v. Educate Employees:
Provide regular training to employees on data security best practices, including how to identify and report potential security incidents.

vi. Collaborate with Vendors:
Work closely with third-party vendors to ensure that they

adhere to your organization's data security standards and have robust incident response plans in place.

In today's business landscape, data breaches are an ever-present threat. By implementing a comprehensive data breach response plan, organizations can effectively manage the risks associated with data breaches and protect their assets, reputation, and stakeholders. By following best practices and continuously evaluating and improving their data security measures, businesses can enhance their resilience and maintain the trust of their customers and partners.

c. Cyber Risk Assessment and Management

Cyber risk assessment and management is a critical process for modern businesses to identify, analyze, and mitigate potential cybersecurity threats. It involves a structured approach to ensure organizations can effectively protect their digital assets and maintain business continuity in the face of evolving cyber risks.

Key Steps in Cyber Risk Assessment and Management
   i. Identifying Risks:
      This initial step involves a comprehensive understanding of the organization's IT environment, including data, networks, systems, and third-party components. It's about measuring the value and importance of different assets and understanding where breaches could potentially originate.
   ii. Assessing and Analyzing Risks:
      After identifying risks, the next step is to assess their severity by evaluating the likelihood of occurrence and potential impact. This includes analyzing risks based on historical occurrences and determining the organization's acceptable level of risk tolerance.
   iii. Prioritizing and Responding to Risks:
      Risks are prioritized to ensure that the most significant threats are addressed swiftly, based on their potential impact.

Organizations must decide on their appetite for risk, which could include treating, tolerating, terminating, or transferring the risk. This decision-making process involves considering various mitigation strategies to address the identified risks effectively.

iv. Monitoring and Reviewing:
Continuous monitoring of risk and controls is essential. This involves regularly reviewing the cyber risk management activities and performance to ensure that controls are effective in mitigating risks. Organizations must also stay current on all cybersecurity risks by documenting all risks in a risk register and reviewing it regularly.

v. Continuous Improvement:
Learning and improving based on the outcomes of the cyber risk management process is vital. Fostering a culture of continuous learning and improvement helps the organization stay ahead of potential cybersecurity threats.

The Role of a Cybersecurity Risk Manager

In the modern digital landscape, the role of a cybersecurity risk manager is crucial in ensuring the security and resilience of organizations against evolving cyber threats. Their mission involves a multifaceted approach, encompassing identification, analysis, assessment, estimation, mitigation, and communication of risks.

Key responsibilities of a cybersecurity risk manager include:
i. Developing a comprehensive cybersecurity risk management strategy tailored to the organization's unique needs
ii. Managing an inventory of organizational assets and understanding their value and vulnerabilities
iii. Identifying and assessing cybersecurity threats and vulnerabilities within ICT systems
iv. Proposing appropriate risk treatment options, such as security controls, mitigation strategies, and avoidance techniques

v. Monitoring and ensuring the effectiveness of implemented controls and adjusting mitigation strategies as needed

Challenges in Modern Cyber Risk Management
Managing cyber risk across the enterprise is harder than ever due to several factors:
i. Explosion of cloud services and third-party vendors:
Organizations share confidential information with numerous third parties, making it challenging for IT security teams to manage complex infrastructures and vendor risk.
ii. Growing number of laws and regulations:
Organizations face increasing accountability for how confidential data must be protected, including third parties processing data on their behalf.
iii. COVID-19 pandemic and recession:
Remote work, unsecured networks, scrambled security protocols, and budget/staffing cuts have increased responsibility for enterprises with fewer resources.

To navigate these complexities, organizations need to employ a comprehensive risk management process, utilize analytics and collaboration tools, and adopt third-party risk management frameworks.

In conclusion, cyber risk assessment and management is a crucial process for modern businesses to protect their digital assets, ensure compliance, and maintain business continuity in the face of evolving cyber threats. By implementing a structured approach and leveraging the expertise of cybersecurity risk managers, organizations can build robust security postures and adapt to the changing threat landscape.

d. Role of IT in Risk Management
IT plays a critical role in modern risk management for businesses. Here are the key ways IT supports effective risk management:

i. IT enables timely and accurate risk information.
   IT systems collect, process, and report risk data, allowing risk managers to make informed decisions. Without robust IT infrastructure, risk management would be manual and inefficient.
ii. IT automates risk processes.
   Workflow tools, dashboards, and analytics powered by IT streamline risk identification, assessment, mitigation, and monitoring. Automation reduces human error and improves consistency in risk management.
iii. IT enables proactive risk management.
   Predictive analytics and AI/ML models leverage big data to anticipate emerging risks. This allows businesses to get ahead of potential threats and vulnerabilities. Real-time risk monitoring is also enabled by IT.
iv. IT improves risk communication.
   Collaboration tools and reporting systems facilitate sharing risk information across the organization. This aligns risk management with business objectives and ensures risks are managed holistically.
v. IT enhances risk controls.
   Technical controls like firewalls, encryption, and multi-factor authentication implemented by IT teams directly mitigate IT risks. Effective IT security is foundational to managing cyber, data, and operational risks.

In summary, IT is deeply integrated into all aspects of risk management today. From data to analytics to controls, IT underpins the people, processes, and technologies that allow organizations to identify, assess, mitigate, and monitor risks in a rapidly changing business environment. Investing in IT capabilities is crucial for modern risk management.

e. Emerging Technologies
   Emerging technologies are revolutionizing the field of risk

management, enabling businesses to proactively identify, assess, and mitigate risks in an increasingly complex and dynamic environment. Here are some key emerging technologies transforming modern risk management:

i. Artificial Intelligence (AI) and Machine Learning (ML)

AI and ML are powerful tools for risk management, allowing organizations to analyze vast amounts of data, identify patterns, and make data-driven decisions. These technologies enable real-time risk assessment, anomaly detection, and automated risk management processes, enhancing efficiency and accuracy.

AI algorithms can assess risks, forecast potential threats, and inform decision-making processes.

ii. Internet of Things (IoT)

IoT technology is transforming risk management by providing real-time data from connected devices and sensors. IoT sensors can monitor equipment performance, inventory levels, and supply chain operations, alerting managers to potential risks before they occur. This data is invaluable for staying ahead of potential risks and making informed decisions.

iii. Cybersecurity

With the increasing threat of cyber-attacks, robust cybersecurity measures are crucial for risk management. Advanced cybersecurity technologies, such as threat intelligence, encryption, and behavioral analytics, help identify and mitigate cyber risks. Staying informed about the latest cyber threats and adopting robust security protocols is essential for effective cybersecurity.

iv. Big Data Analytics

Big data analytics enables organizations to identify trends, forecast risks, and inform decision-making processes. Advanced analytics tools can sift through large datasets to uncover patterns and correlations that might go unnoticed otherwise. This can help businesses predict customer behavior, assess market trends, and identify operational risks.

v. Blockchain

   Blockchain technology provides secure, transparent, and tamper-proof records, making it an ideal tool for managing transactions, contracts, and data securely. In risk management, blockchain can enhance transparency and traceability, mitigating risks associated with fraud, counterfeiting, and compliance.

To successfully adopt these emerging technologies, businesses need a strategic approach that considers the specific risks and challenges of their industry. Conducting thorough due diligence, structuring payments to incentivize technology success, and negotiating favorable liability and performance guarantee provisions are key risk mitigation strategies.

Embracing emerging technologies in risk management is crucial for businesses to stay ahead in the ever-changing digital landscape. However, technology alone is not enough; it must be complemented by a holistic risk management approach, strong leadership commitment, and a focus on building secure, compliant, and resilient organizations.

10 OPERATIONAL RISK MANAGEMENT

Operational risk management is a critical component of modern risk management in business. It involves identifying, assessing, and mitigating risks that can disrupt an organization's operations and prevent it from achieving its objectives.

In today's rapidly evolving business landscape, organizations face a wide range of operational risks, such as system failures, human errors, fraud, and natural disasters. These risks can lead to financial losses, reputational damage, and regulatory penalties if not managed effectively.

To address these challenges, organizations are adopting a risk-based mindset towards operational risk management. This approach prioritizes understanding and managing risks based on their potential impact on the organization, rather than relying on a one-size-fits-all compliance checklist.

Key elements of effective operational risk management include:

i. Clearly defined roles and responsibilities for everyone involved in the risk management process
ii. Engagement with stakeholders to gather information about potential risks and mitigation strategies
iii. Thorough risk assessments using a combination of qualitative and quantitative techniques
iv. Development of realistic and effective mitigation strategies that align with the organization's goals and resources
v. Regular monitoring and review of risks and mitigation strategies
vi. Fostering a risk-aware culture within the organization

By adopting a risk-based mindset and implementing these best practices, organizations can better protect their operations, safeguard their reputation, and create value for their stakeholders in the long run.

a. Business Continuity Planning

Business Continuity Planning (BCP) is a critical component of modern risk management in business. It involves identifying potential threats to an organization and developing strategies to mitigate the impact of those threats on business operations.

BCP ensures that an organization can maintain critical functions or return to normal operations as quickly and smoothly as possible in the event of a disruption.

Key Elements of Business Continuity Planning

i. Resilience:
Building a robust foundation by designing and implementing fail-safes within the organization's critical functions and infrastructures to withstand disruptions before they occur. This includes measures such as diversifying supply chains, implementing backup power supplies, and ensuring redundant IT systems.

ii. Response:
Developing contingency plans that outline the actions to take in response to various disruptive scenarios. These plans should be regularly tested and updated to ensure their effectiveness.

iii. Recovery:
Establishing strategies to restore normal operations as quickly as possible after a disruption. This may involve alternative work arrangements, such as remote work or temporary relocation.

Integrating BCP with Enterprise Risk Management

Effective risk management requires the integration of BCP with Enterprise Risk Management (ERM). ERM involves identifying, assessing, and prioritizing potential threats that could disrupt normal operations. By combining BCP and ERM, organizations can develop a unified risk management strategy that allows them to anticipate issues, make informed decisions, and enhance resilience in the face of unexpected disruptions.

Cultivating a Culture of Preparedness

Fostering a culture of preparedness is essential for the success of BCP. This involves regular training for employees, open communication with stakeholders, continuous improvement of plans, and empowerment of employees to contribute to continuity strategies. By engaging employees and promoting a proactive mindset, organizations can enhance their resilience and responsiveness to potential threats.

Adapting to Modern Risks

The landscape of business continuity risks is ever-changing, driven by technological advancements, evolving threats, and an increasingly interconnected global economy. Organizations must be agile and adaptable, ready to face whatever challenges come their way. By understanding the nature of these risks, implementing a mix of preventive, detective, and corrective controls, and fostering a proactive culture of preparedness, organizations can navigate these complexities effectively.

In conclusion, Business Continuity Planning is a crucial aspect of modern risk management in business. By identifying potential threats, developing robust contingency plans, and fostering a culture of preparedness, organizations can enhance their resilience and ensure the continuity of their operations in the face of disruptions. Integrating BCP with Enterprise Risk

Management provides a comprehensive approach to managing risks and enables organizations to adapt to the evolving business landscape.

b. Disaster Recovery Planning

Disaster recovery planning is a critical component of modern risk management for businesses. It involves developing a comprehensive strategy to protect an organization's critical assets, respond effectively to incidents, and ensure business continuity in the face of various threats.

Key Steps in Disaster Recovery Planning

i. Risk assessment and business impact analysis:
Identify potential risks, both natural and human-made, that could disrupt business operations. Assess the impact of these risks on critical systems, data, and processes.

ii. Establishing recovery objectives:
Define recovery point objectives (RPO) and recovery time objectives (RTO) for each critical system. RPO determines the acceptable data loss, while RTO specifies the maximum downtime.

iii. Developing recovery strategies:
Implement strategies to recover critical systems and data, such as offsite backups, redundant infrastructure, and failover mechanisms.

iv. Continuity planning:
Develop plans to maintain business functions and recover essential components of the IT environment. This may involve having teams work from alternate sites or using cloud-based disaster recovery solutions.

v. Testing and maintenance:
Regularly test the disaster recovery plan to ensure its effectiveness and update it as needed to address changes in the business environment and evolving threats.

Importance of Disaster Recovery Planning

Disaster recovery planning is crucial for business continuity in today's challenging risk environment. Outages caused by threats like ransomware, human errors, or natural disasters can seriously impact a company's bottom line and even put it out of business. Without a comprehensive disaster recovery plan, organizations are vulnerable to extended downtime, data loss, and financial repercussions. Effective planning helps minimize the impact of disasters, maintain customer trust, and ensure regulatory compliance.

Challenges and Solutions
Developing and maintaining an effective disaster recovery plan can be complex and costly. Challenges include insufficient resources, limited testing, high expenses associated with DR technology, and slow response times. To overcome these challenges, businesses should allocate sufficient resources for an effective DR plan, establish routine testing schedules, and consider cloud-based disaster recovery solutions like Disaster Recovery as a Service (DRaaS). DRaaS allows organizations to replicate and store critical data, applications, and systems in the cloud, enabling rapid failover and recovery in the event of a disaster. It simplifies the complexities of traditional disaster recovery planning and provides scalability, cost-effectiveness, and increased reliability.

In conclusion, disaster recovery planning is a crucial aspect of modern risk management for businesses. By following best practices, overcoming challenges, and leveraging cloud-based solutions, organizations can protect their critical assets, maintain business continuity, and ensure long-term success in the face of evolving threats.

c. Crisis Management
Crisis management is a critical component of modern risk management for businesses. It involves identifying potential threats to an organization and its stakeholders, and developing effective response strategies to mitigate the impact of these threats. Even well-managed businesses can face crises due to external factors like natural disasters, security breaches, or damaging

rumors, as well as internal factors such as employee misconduct or poor customer service. Crisis management helps organizations anticipate and plan for these unexpected events, enabling them to adapt and survive when a crisis does occur.

The key elements of an effective crisis management framework include:

i. Crisis identification:
   Establishing early warning systems and a triggering mechanism to promptly identify and declare a crisis.
ii. Contingency planning:
   Maintaining a comprehensive inventory of detailed contingency plans for various types and magnitudes of risks.
iii. Crisis governance:
   Implementing a streamlined decision-making process, similar to military-style governance, to enable swift responses during a crisis.
iv. Management information (MI) systems:
   Developing flexible MI systems that can rapidly process relevant data to address evolving crisis situations.
v. Crisis communication:
   Establishing clear crisis communication principles and plans for internal and external stakeholders.

Regular crisis management exercises, such as war game simulations, are crucial for testing and refining crisis mitigation strategies and training key personnel.

Crisis management is distinct from risk management, as it focuses on reacting to negative events as they occur, while risk management involves planning for potential future events. However, both are essential components of modern risk management, as they help organizations anticipate, prepare for, and respond to threats that could disrupt their operations and damage their reputation.

By implementing a robust crisis management framework, businesses can better protect themselves and their stakeholders from the potentially devastating consequences of unexpected crises.

d. Supply Chain Risk Management (SCRM)

Supply Chain Risk Management (SCRM) is a critical strategy for modern businesses to identify, assess, and mitigate risks across their supply chains.

In today's complex and interconnected business landscape, supply chains face a myriad of potential disruptions, including natural disasters, cyber-attacks, financial instability of suppliers, and geopolitical tensions.

A comprehensive SCRM approach involves several key elements:

i. Risk Identification and Assessment

The first step is to identify and document potential risks across the supply chain. This includes gathering data from various sources, such as supplier financial reports, news articles, and internal operational data. Advanced analytics and digital tools like supply chain control towers can help analyze this data to assess the likelihood and impact of different risk scenarios.

ii. Risk Mitigation Strategies

Once risks are identified, organizations need to develop tailored mitigation strategies. This may involve diversifying supplier base, implementing backup plans, or investing in more resilient technologies. A closed-loop approach that continuously monitors performance and adapts strategies based on feedback is crucial for agility.

iii. Supplier Risk Management

Supplier risk is a critical component of SCRM. Robust supplier onboarding processes, regular risk assessments, and continuous monitoring are essential to ensure the financial stability and compliance of third-party partners. Leveraging data science and analytics platforms can automate and streamline supplier risk management.

iv. Cross-Functional Collaboration

Effective SCRM requires close collaboration between various departments, including procurement, logistics, IT, and risk management. A centralized governance structure and clear communication channels are key to aligning objectives and coordinating risk mitigation efforts.

v. Digital Transformation

Investing in digital technologies is a game-changer for SCRM. Tools like digital supply chain twins, control towers, and predictive analytics enable organizations to simulate scenarios, gain end-to-end visibility, and make data-driven decisions. However, according to a 2022 article, 63% of companies still do not use any technology to monitor their supply chain performance.

In conclusion, embracing a proactive and technology-driven approach to SCRM is no longer a choice but a necessity for modern businesses.

By identifying risks, implementing mitigation strategies, and leveraging digital tools, organizations can build resilient and agile supply chains capable of withstanding disruptions and seizing opportunities in an increasingly volatile business environment.

11 STRATEGIC RISK MANAGEMENT

Strategic risk management is a critical component of modern business risk management. It involves identifying, assessing, and mitigating risks that are directly tied to a company's strategic objectives and long-term success.

Key Aspects of Strategic Risk Management
 i. Identifying strategic risks:
    This includes analyzing both internal and external factors that could impact the company's ability to achieve its goals, such as market shifts, technological advancements, and regulatory changes.
 ii. Assessing strategic risks:
    Evaluating the likelihood and potential impact of identified risks allows businesses to prioritize their efforts and allocate resources effectively.
 iii. Developing mitigation strategies:
    Businesses should explore various options to mitigate strategic risks, such as risk avoidance, risk transfer, or risk acceptance.
 iv. Integrating risk management into business strategy:
    Effective strategic risk management requires seamless integration into the overall business strategy, ensuring that risk considerations guide decision-making at all levels.
 v. Leveraging technology and data analytics:
    Modern businesses can enhance their strategic risk management by utilizing data analytics and artificial intelligence to identify trends, forecast potential risks, and make data-driven decisions.
 vi. Continuous monitoring and adaptation:
    Strategic risk management is an ongoing process that requires constant vigilance. Regular monitoring of risks and the ability to adapt strategies accordingly are hallmarks of successful risk management.

Benefits of Strategic Risk Management
i. Improved decision-making:
By considering potential risks and their impact, businesses can make more informed and strategic decisions.
ii. Enhanced resilience:
Effective strategic risk management helps businesses anticipate and mitigate potential threats, increasing their ability to withstand unexpected challenges.
iii. Competitive advantage:
Companies that proactively manage strategic risks are better positioned to capitalize on opportunities and gain a competitive edge in the market.
iv. Sustainable growth:
By aligning risk management with organizational objectives, businesses can ensure long-term success and sustainable growth.

In conclusion, strategic risk management is a crucial aspect of modern business risk management. By embracing a proactive and integrated approach to identifying, assessing, and mitigating strategic risks, businesses can navigate the dynamic and ever-evolving business landscape with confidence and achieve their long-term goals.

a. Scenario Planning

Scenario planning is a crucial tool for modern risk management in business. It involves envisioning multiple plausible future scenarios and developing strategies to navigate them effectively. By embracing uncertainty and exploring a range of potential outcomes, scenario planning enables organizations to:

i. Mitigate risks:
Scenario planning helps identify and address uncertainties, enhancing an organization's resilience and ability to navigate turbulent times.
ii. Maintain strategic flexibility:
In a dynamic business environment, scenario planning fosters agility in decision-making and execution by allowing organizations to adapt their strategies to different future scenarios.

iii. Inform decision-making:
By considering various potential futures, scenario planning provides a more comprehensive understanding of the business landscape, leading to better-informed decisions.

The scenario planning process typically involves the following steps:

i. Setting objectives:
Defining the purpose of scenario planning, such as identifying threats, developing new strategies, or testing existing ones.

ii. Determining key factors:
Identifying critical internal and external factors that could impact the organization's performance.

iii. Exploring future trends:
Researching and analyzing how the driving forces behind these key factors might evolve over time.

iv. Developing plausible scenarios:
Creating detailed narratives that describe potential future states, focusing on the interplay of key factors and driving forces.

v. Implication analysis:
Assessing the implications of each scenario for the organization, including risks and opportunities.

vi. Strategy formulation:
Developing flexible strategies to manage identified risks and capitalize on opportunities.

vii. Implementation and monitoring:
Putting the strategies into action and regularly reviewing and updating them to reflect the changing landscape.

Scenario planning can be applied in various forms, such as quantitative scenarios (financial models), operational scenarios (exploring the immediate impact of events), normative scenarios (describing preferred end states), and strategic management scenarios (exploring the broader environment).

By incorporating scenario planning into their risk management strategies, organizations can navigate the uncertainties of the modern business landscape more effectively. It encourages strategic thinking, promotes resilience, and helps organizations move beyond simple risk mitigation towards a more dynamic and adaptive approach to risk management.

b. Competitive Risk Analysis

Competitive risk analysis is a crucial component of modern risk management for businesses operating in today's dynamic and competitive landscape. It involves identifying, assessing, and mitigating risks that arise from the actions and strategies of competitors. By proactively analyzing competitive risks, businesses can gain a strategic advantage, adapt to market changes, and safeguard their market position.

Identifying Competitive Risks

The first step in competitive risk analysis is to identify potential risks that may arise from competitor activities. This includes:

i. Analyzing competitors' product roadmaps and innovation pipelines to anticipate new product launches or feature enhancements that could disrupt your market position
ii. Monitoring competitors' pricing strategies and assessing the impact of potential price wars or undercutting on your profitability
iii. Identifying competitors' expansion plans, such as entering new markets or targeting your customer segments, which could lead to increased competition
iv. Assessing the risk of competitors forming strategic alliances or partnerships that could strengthen their market position relative to yours.

Assessing Competitive Risks

Once potential competitive risks have been identified, the next step is to assess their likelihood and potential impact on your business.

This involves:
i. Conducting market research to gauge customer preferences, loyalty, and willingness to switch to competitors
ii. Analyzing competitors' financial strength, market share, and resources to determine their ability to invest in and sustain competitive initiatives
iii. Evaluating the potential impact of competitive risks on your revenue, market share, and profitability
iv. Prioritizing risks based on their likelihood and potential impact to focus your risk management efforts

Mitigating Competitive Risks
To mitigate competitive risks, businesses should develop and implement strategies to maintain their competitive edge and adapt to changing market conditions. This may include:
i. Investing in continuous innovation to stay ahead of competitors and offer unique value propositions to customers
ii. Differentiating your products or services through superior quality, customer service, or brand positioning
iii. Pursuing strategic partnerships or acquisitions to strengthen your market position and access new technologies or customer segments
iv. Monitoring and responding to competitors' actions in a timely manner to minimize the impact on your business

Monitoring and Adapting
Competitive risk management is an ongoing process that requires continuous monitoring and adaptation. Businesses should regularly review their competitive risk assessments and adjust their strategies accordingly. This involves:
i. Tracking competitors' actions and market performance through regular market intelligence gathering
ii. Analyzing the effectiveness of your risk mitigation strategies and making necessary adjustments

iii. Fostering a culture of innovation and adaptability within your organization to respond quickly to competitive threats

In conclusion, competitive risk analysis is a critical component of modern risk management for businesses. By identifying, assessing, and mitigating competitive risks, businesses can maintain their competitive edge, adapt to market changes, and drive sustainable growth in today's dynamic business environment.

c. Mergers and Acquisitions Risk
Mergers and acquisitions (M&A) transactions carry significant risks that must be carefully managed to ensure a successful outcome. Some of the key risks include:
   i. Integration Risks
      Integration risks are among the most significant in M&A, as they can cause operational, cultural, or organizational disruptions if not properly managed. A well-designed integration plan and change management process is critical. Many companies establish a formal integration team to handle this process and ensure smooth communication throughout the transition. Retaining key employees is an essential element of the integration plan. A well-structured retention plan can help maintain crucial talent and expertise that contributes to the success of the newly merged entity.
   ii. Financial Risks
      Financial risks can stem from overpaying for the target company, unanticipated expenses, or due diligence errors. To mitigate these risks, companies should assess and reevaluate the target's profitability compared to the purchase price to ensure reasonable and well-informed valuations. Maintaining a strong financial infrastructure through strategies like physical concentration, notional pooling, and overlay structures can help ensure the merged entity maintains liquidity and financial stability.

iii. Regulatory and Legal Risks
Mergers and acquisitions have regulatory aspects that must be attended to avoid legal issues, such as antitrust concerns. Companies must understand local laws and regulations and consider tax implications as part of their M&A strategy.

iv. Failure to Achieve Synergies
One of the primary motivations for M&A is to achieve synergies and create value. However, many deals fail to capitalize on these synergies due to poor planning, execution, or integration. A clear understanding of the expected synergies and a plan to realize them is crucial.

v. Cultural Differences
Differences in corporate culture between the acquiring and target companies can create challenges in integration and lead to employee retention issues. Proactive communication and a focus on cultural alignment can help mitigate this risk.

To effectively manage M&A risks, companies should:
i. Conduct thorough due diligence to identify potential risks and liabilities
ii. Develop a comprehensive integration plan with clear roles and responsibilities
iii. Maintain open and transparent communication with stakeholders throughout the process
iv. Establish a dedicated risk management function to identify, assess, and mitigate risks
v. Continuously monitor and adapt risk management strategies as the integration progresses

By proactively identifying and managing these risks, companies can improve their chances of a successful M&A transaction and create long-term value for shareholders.

d. Innovation and Risk
Innovation and risk management are closely intertwined in modern

business. Effective risk management is crucial for businesses to successfully pursue innovation and achieve sustainable growth in a dynamic and competitive environment.

Innovation involves taking risks to create new or improved products, services, processes, or business models that meet evolving customer needs. However, innovation also brings uncertainty, complexity, and potential threats that need to be managed proactively. This is where innovation risk management comes into play.

Innovation risk management involves systematically identifying, assessing, prioritizing, mitigating, monitoring, and communicating the potential risks and opportunities associated with innovation projects.

By adopting a structured approach to innovation risk management, businesses can:
i. Enhance the quality and efficiency of the innovation process
ii. Increase the likelihood of innovation success by aligning with business strategy
iii. Reduce the negative impacts of innovation failure by anticipating scenarios
iv. Foster a culture of innovation by encouraging creativity and learning

Implementing effective innovation risk management requires following key steps:
i. Define the scope and objectives of the innovation project and establish risk appetite
ii. Identify sources and types of risks that can affect the innovation project
iii. Assess the probability and impact of each risk and rank them by severity
iv. Develop and implement risk mitigation strategies such as

       avoiding, reducing, transferring or accepting risks
v. Monitor and review the risk status and adjust mitigation plans as needed
vi. Communicate risk information to relevant stakeholders

The benefits of integrating innovation risk management into business strategy are numerous:
i. Facilitates problem-solving and enhances customer experience
ii. Boosts adaptability to unexpected changes and market shifts
iii. Raises competitiveness by enabling structured, sustainable innovation
iv. Enables informed strategic decisions based on risk-reward tradeoffs
v. Protects reputation by proactively managing risks
vi. Ensures regulatory compliance and market responsiveness
vii. Contributes to financial performance by avoiding pitfalls of failed innovations

In conclusion, innovation and risk management are not opposing forces, but rather complementary elements that enable businesses to thrive amidst uncertainty.

By embracing innovation risk management as a strategic discipline, companies can confidently pursue cutting-edge ideas while maintaining operational stability and financial performance.

The integration of data analytics and technology further empowers businesses to make informed risk-based decisions and adapt to the rapidly evolving business landscape.

12 REPUTATION RISK MANAGEMENT

Reputation risk management is a critical component of modern risk management for businesses. It involves identifying, assessing, and mitigating risks that can harm a company's reputation and public perception.

In today's digital age, a company's reputation can be damaged quickly through negative publicity, unethical behavior, or failure to meet stakeholder expectations. Reputation is one of the most valuable assets a business possesses, as it impacts customer trust, employee satisfaction, and overall financial performance. Effective reputation risk management requires a proactive and comprehensive approach.

It starts with assessing potential sources of reputational damage, such as process failures, employee misconduct, or issues with suppliers and partners. Companies must then develop strategies to mitigate these risks, including establishing strong governance structures, creating crisis management plans, and educating employees on the importance of reputation.

Monitoring stakeholder perceptions, industry trends, and emerging risks is also crucial for managing reputational risks. Companies should regularly assess their reputation and make adjustments to their risk management strategies as needed.

By prioritizing reputation risk management, modern businesses can protect their most valuable asset, build trust with stakeholders, and position themselves for long-term success. It is an essential component of a comprehensive risk management framework in today's fast-paced and increasingly complex business environment.

a. Media and Public Relations

   Media and public relations play a crucial role in modern risk management for businesses. In today's interconnected world, where information spreads rapidly, effective communication is essential for mitigating risks and safeguarding an organization's reputation.

   i. The Evolving Role of PR in Risk Management

      Public relations strategies have evolved to keep pace with the changing business landscape. Modern PR professionals are at the forefront of anticipating and managing crises, leveraging digital channels and social media to engage stakeholders in real-time. Proactive communication and transparent responses during challenging times can make or break a company's reputation.

   ii. Reputation Management and Crisis Communication

      Reputation management has become paramount in the age of instant information sharing. Businesses must proactively safeguard their brand image and be prepared to respond swiftly to potential crises. PR experts employ data-driven approaches to assess the impact of their efforts, using metrics such as reach, engagement, and sentiment analysis to fine-tune their strategies.

   iii. Stakeholder Engagement and Media Relations

      Effective stakeholder engagement goes beyond customers and investors, encompassing employees, communities, and activists. PR professionals skillfully navigate the varied media landscape, which now includes traditional outlets, online publications, bloggers, and influencers. By building and maintaining strong relationships with all stakeholders, organizations can foster trust and loyalty, contributing to a positive brand image.

iv. The Intersection of PR and Risk Management
Public relations and risk management are inextricably linked. Effective PR is an integral part of risk management, as it helps shape public perception and maintain a favorable reputation. Conversely, a strong reputation bolsters the credibility of an organization's communication efforts.

In conclusion, media and public relations are essential components of modern risk management. By embracing strategic communication, reputation management, and stakeholder engagement, businesses can navigate the complexities of the modern landscape, build trust, and ensure long-term success.

b. Stakeholder Engagement
Stakeholder engagement is a critical component of effective risk management in today's business landscape. By actively involving stakeholders in the risk management process, organizations can gain valuable insights, foster collaboration, and make informed decisions to mitigate potential threats and capitalize on opportunities.

Here are some key aspects of stakeholder engagement for modern risk management:

i. Identifying Key Stakeholders
The first step in stakeholder engagement is to identify all relevant individuals and groups who may be affected by or have an impact on the organization's risks. This includes internal stakeholders such as employees, management, and board members, as well as external stakeholders like customers, suppliers, investors, and regulatory bodies.

ii. Assessing Stakeholder Needs and Expectations
Once key stakeholders have been identified, it is essential to understand their needs, concerns, and expectations regarding risk management. This can be done through surveys,

interviews, and workshops, allowing stakeholders to voice their perspectives and provide valuable insights.

iii. Communicating Effectively
Effective communication is crucial for successful stakeholder engagement in risk management. Organizations should establish clear and transparent channels of communication, regularly updating stakeholders on risk-related issues and decisions. This fosters trust, collaboration, and a shared understanding of the organization's risk management approach.

iv. Involving Stakeholders in Decision-Making
By actively involving stakeholders in the decision-making process, organizations can gain a broader perspective on risk-related issues and challenges. This diversity of viewpoints enables informed decision-making, leading to better outcomes and solutions.

v. Monitoring and Reassessing Risks
Stakeholder engagement should be an ongoing process throughout the risk management lifecycle. Organizations should regularly monitor and reassess risks, engaging with stakeholders to ensure that their concerns and expectations are being addressed. This adaptability allows organizations to respond quickly to changing circumstances and emerging threats.

vi. Fostering a Risk-Aware Culture
Effective stakeholder engagement in risk management requires a cultural shift within the organization. By championing the importance of risk management at the leadership level and engaging all stakeholders in the process, organizations can foster a risk-aware culture that values proactive measures, continuous assessment, and informed decision-making.

In conclusion, stakeholder engagement is a crucial aspect of modern risk management. By identifying key stakeholders, assessing their needs and expectations, communicating effectively, involving them in decision-making, and fostering a risk-aware culture, organizations can enhance their ability to identify, assess, and mitigate risks while capitalizing on opportunities for growth and success.

c. Crisis Communication Plans

Crisis communication plans are essential for modern businesses to effectively manage risks and protect their reputation. In today's rapidly changing and interconnected world, organizations face a wide range of potential crises, from natural disasters and cybersecurity breaches to product recalls and reputational issues. A well-designed crisis communication plan provides a structured approach to responding to unexpected events, ensuring that information is disseminated promptly, accurately, and consistently to stakeholders. By having a plan in place, businesses can mitigate the negative impact of a crisis, maintain operational continuity, and safeguard their reputation.

Key elements of an effective crisis communication plan include:

i. Risk assessment:
   Identifying potential risks and vulnerabilities specific to the organization.
ii. Communication protocols:
   Establishing clear guidelines for sharing information internally and externally.
iii. Stakeholder identification:
   Determining key stakeholders, including employees, customers, media, and regulatory agencies.
iv. Messaging frameworks:
   Developing pre-approved messaging templates for different crisis scenarios.

v. Monitoring systems:
Implementing procedures to monitor media, social media, and other information sources related to the crisis.
vi. Training and drills:
Conducting regular training sessions and crisis simulations to test communication protocols and identify areas for improvement.

By investing in a dedicated crisis communications team and leveraging technology tools for media monitoring and social media analysis, organizations can enhance their ability to navigate uncertain periods successfully. Effective crisis communication not only mitigates immediate reputational risks but also fosters long-term stakeholder trust and loyalty.

In conclusion, a robust crisis communication plan is a critical component of modern risk management in business. By proactively assessing risks, establishing clear communication protocols, and engaging stakeholders effectively, organizations can enhance their resilience and safeguard their reputation in the face of unexpected challenges.

d. Social Media Risk
Social media risk management is a critical component of modern business risk management. As social media has become an integral part of how companies communicate with customers, employees, and the public, it has also introduced new risks that must be proactively managed.

Some of the key social media risks businesses face include:
i. Reputational risk:
Negative reviews, comments or scandals going viral on social media can cause significant damage to a company's reputation.
ii. Security risks:
Unauthorized access to sensitive information like customer

data through hacked social media accounts can lead to data breaches and loss of trust.
iii. Compliance risks:
Failure to adhere to legal, regulatory and platform guidelines around privacy, advertising, and content can result in investigations and penalties.
iv. Operational risks:
Social media blunders, inadequate training, and technical issues can disrupt business operations and effectiveness of social media strategies.
v. Crisis communication risks:
Challenges in managing communication during a crisis or negative event on social media.

To manage these risks, companies need to have a comprehensive social media risk management plan in place. This typically involves:
i. Identifying social media goals and risks for the organization
ii. Establishing a clear social media policy and guidelines
iii. Implementing security measures like strong passwords and two-factor authentication
iv. Educating employees on social media best practices and risks
v. Monitoring social media conversations and responding appropriately to criticism
vi. Having a crisis communication plan ready to address negative events quickly and transparently

Staying on top of evolving social media trends is also key, as authenticity, crisis management, and the use of influencers and data will be critical in 2024. By proactively identifying, assessing and mitigating social media risks, businesses can harness the power of social media to engage customers and grow, while safeguarding their reputation and operations. A well-designed social media risk management strategy is now an essential part of modern corporate risk management.

13 RISK MANAGEMENT TOOLS AND SOFTWARE

Risk management tools and software provide businesses with a structured approach to managing risks, enabling them to proactively identify, analyze, and respond to potential threats. These tools offer a range of features and functionalities, such as risk assessment matrices, risk registers, and risk mitigation planning, to help organizations effectively manage risks across various domains, including financial, operational, strategic, and compliance.

Benefits of Using Risk Management Tools and Software

i. Improved risk identification and assessment:
Risk management tools and software provide a systematic approach to identifying and assessing risks, allowing organizations to prioritize and focus on the most critical threats.

ii. Enhanced decision-making:
By providing data-driven insights and risk analysis, these tools support informed decision-making, enabling organizations to make well-informed choices that balance risk and reward.

iii. Streamlined risk management processes:
Risk management tools automate various processes, such as risk reporting, monitoring, and communication, reducing manual effort and ensuring consistency across the organization.

iv. Increased efficiency and productivity:
By automating repetitive tasks and providing real-time risk data, risk management tools and software help organizations optimize their risk management processes, leading to increased efficiency and productivity.

v. Better compliance and governance:
Many risk management tools and software incorporate industry-specific regulations and best practices, helping organizations maintain compliance and adhere to governance standards.

vi. Improved risk culture:
By providing a centralized platform for risk management, these tools foster a culture of risk awareness and accountability throughout the organization.

Types of Risk Management Tools and Software

i. Risk assessment and analysis tools:
These tools help organizations identify, assess, and prioritize risks based on their likelihood and impact. Examples include risk assessment matrices, heat maps, and risk registers.

ii. Risk mitigation and control tools:
These tools support the implementation and monitoring of risk mitigation strategies, such as risk response plans, control libraries, and risk treatment workflows.

iii. Risk reporting and dashboard tools:
These tools provide real-time risk data and insights through interactive dashboards, reports, and visualizations, enabling organizations to monitor and communicate risk information effectively.

iv. Compliance and regulatory tools:
These tools help organizations manage compliance-related risks by providing features such as regulatory libraries, compliance checklists, and audit management functionalities.

v. Enterprise risk management (ERM) platforms:
ERM platforms offer a comprehensive solution for managing risks across the entire organization, integrating various risk management processes and data sources into a single platform.

vi. Specialized risk management tools:
Depending on the industry or specific risk domain, organizations may use specialized tools, such as financial risk management software, project risk management tools, or cybersecurity risk assessment platforms.

Risk management tools and software have become essential for modern businesses seeking to navigate the complex and ever-evolving risk landscape. By leveraging these tools, organizations can enhance their risk management capabilities, make informed decisions, and maintain a competitive edge in their respective markets. As technology continues to advance, the field of risk management tools and software will likely evolve, offering even more sophisticated solutions to help organizations manage risks effectively and efficiently.

a. Risk Management Information Systems (RMIS)

A Risk Management Information System (RMIS) is a software platform that helps organizations collect, manage, analyze, and report on risk, claims, and safety information. It consolidates data from various sources into a centralized system, providing a clear view of an organization's risks, relationships, and impact.

Key features and benefits of a RMIS include:
i. Automating workflows and streamlining routine tasks to save time and reduce errors
ii. Facilitating advanced reporting and analytics to identify trends, emerging risks, and cost-saving opportunities
iii. Improving data quality and increasing visibility and access to information
iv. Tightening security by storing data in a protected system instead of across different devices and platforms
v. Enabling organizations to make more informed decisions about risk, reducing costs and increasing profitability

A Risk Management Information System (RMIS) can significantly improve the efficiency of risk management in businesses in several key ways:

i. Consolidating data from multiple sources:
A RMIS seamlessly collects and consolidates risk, claims, and safety data from various stakeholders and systems, providing a single view of an organization's risk information. This

eliminates the need to manage data across multiple spreadsheets, documents, and emails.

ii. Automating workflows and streamlining processes:
A RMIS automates and streamlines routine risk management tasks such as renewals, claims management, policy management, incident management, and premium allocations. This saves time and reduces errors compared to manual processes.

iii. Facilitating advanced reporting and analytics:
By consolidating data into a centralized system, a RMIS enables organizations to generate real-time dashboards and reports that provide actionable insights. This allows risk professionals to quickly identify trends, emerging risks, and cost-saving opportunities.

iv. Improving data quality and visibility:
A RMIS stores data in a secure, protected system, ensuring accuracy and increasing visibility and access to information across the organization. Inaccurate data can lead to false findings, so maintaining data quality is crucial.

v. Enabling smarter, faster decisions:
With a RMIS, risk managers can make more informed decisions about risk by understanding the relationships between critical risks and their impact on the organization. This allows them to optimize insurance programs and identify cost-savings opportunities.

vi. Reducing total cost of risk:
By automating processes, improving data quality, and enabling better decision-making, a RMIS can significantly reduce an organization's total cost of risk. It also frees up staff time to focus on higher-value tasks that add real value to the business.

A well-implemented RMIS can streamline workflows, improve data quality, provide actionable insights, and ultimately reduce costs and increase profitability for businesses by turning risk into a strategic advantage. A RMIS is particularly beneficial for organizations with high levels of risk, complex insurance coverage, large quantities of data, or international operations. It helps businesses respond to incidents, avoid them, and factor them into business decisions to facilitate prevention.

By consolidating real-time risk data from multiple sources and understanding the relationships between critical risks, a RMIS allows organizations to optimize their insurance programs, identify cost-savings opportunities, and deliver human-worthy insights from trusted data. This enables risk professionals to make smarter decisions faster and turn risk into a strategic advantage.

b. Predictive Analytics

Predictive analytics has become a crucial tool for effective risk management in modern businesses. By leveraging data, algorithms, and statistical models, organizations can proactively identify, assess, and mitigate potential risks across various domains such as finance, operations, compliance, and strategy.

Predictive analytics enables businesses to forecast future trends, behaviors, and events based on historical data and patterns. This allows companies to anticipate and address risks before they materialize, minimizing their impact and enhancing decision-making processes.

For example, financial institutions can use predictive models to detect fraudulent transactions or predict market fluctuations, while operational risk management can benefit from predicting equipment failures or supply chain disruptions.

The power of predictive analytics lies in its ability to integrate data from multiple sources, including internal, external, and alternative data. By employing advanced techniques such as machine learning, deep learning, and data mining, predictive models can identify complex patterns and relationships within the data. This helps organizations gain a more comprehensive understanding of their risk profile and develop targeted risk mitigation strategies.

Implementing predictive analytics for risk management involves several key steps:
i. Identifying the risk scenarios to monitor
ii. Collecting relevant data for those risks
iii. Choosing suitable predictive models for specific needs
iv. Training the models on the data
v. Validating, monitoring, and executing the models

By following these steps, businesses can leverage predictive insights to improve risk identification and assessment, enhance decision-making, optimize resource allocation, and ultimately drive business transformation. However, effective implementation of predictive analytics for risk management requires a well-defined risk strategy, robust data governance practices, and seamless integration with existing systems. Organizations must also address challenges such as data quality, accessibility, and the siloed approach to risk management.

In conclusion, predictive analytics has revolutionized the way businesses approach risk management. By leveraging data-driven insights, organizations can navigate uncertainties, gain a competitive advantage, and ensure long-term sustainability in today's dynamic business landscape.

c. Software for Risk Assessment and Monitoring
Risk assessment and monitoring software is a critical tool for modern businesses to effectively manage risks across their organization. These specialized software solutions streamline the risk management process by providing a centralized platform to identify, assess, and mitigate risks in real-time.
Key features of risk assessment and monitoring software include:
i. Risk identification and assessment:

The software enables businesses to conduct comprehensive risk assessments by identifying and evaluating risks across various departments and functions. This ensures a holistic view of the organization's risk landscape.

ii. Real-time monitoring and reporting:
Risk assessment software offers real-time monitoring capabilities, allowing businesses to track risks, monitor controls, and receive alerts on potential issues or breaches. This enables proactive risk management and timely decision-making.

iii. Automated workflows and data aggregation:
The software streamlines risk management processes by automating workflows, consolidating data from multiple sources, and providing a centralized platform for managing all aspects of risk. This leads to improved efficiency and effectiveness in addressing risks.

iv. Compliance and governance:
Risk assessment software helps organizations stay compliant by providing tools for tracking regulatory changes, assessing compliance gaps, and implementing necessary controls. It also supports adherence to governance frameworks, ensuring businesses operate within legal and ethical boundaries.

v. Data-driven decision making:
The software leverages data analytics and reporting capabilities to provide valuable insights into risks and their potential impact. This enables businesses to make informed decisions based on data-driven analysis, helping identify emerging risks, evaluate mitigation strategies, and optimize risk management efforts.

vi. Scalability and flexibility:
The best risk assessment software offers scalability and flexibility to accommodate the changing needs of businesses. It can adapt to evolving risk profiles, organizational structures, and industry requirements, ensuring the software remains relevant and effective as the business grows.

By adopting risk assessment and monitoring software, businesses can achieve several benefits, including:

i. Streamlined risk management processes
ii. Comprehensive risk assessment and prioritization
iii. Enhanced compliance and governance
iv. Improved collaboration and communication among stakeholders
v. Scalability and flexibility to adapt to changing business needs

In conclusion, risk assessment and monitoring software is a crucial tool for modern businesses to effectively manage risks and make data-driven decisions.

By leveraging the capabilities of these specialized software solutions, organizations can enhance their risk management strategies, improve operational efficiency, and maintain a competitive edge in today's dynamic business landscape.

14 CASE STUDIES

Here are some key case studies illustrating modern enterprise risk management (ERM) practices in business:

a. Walmart's ERM Framework

Walmart has a well-developed enterprise risk management (ERM) framework that helps the company identify, assess, and mitigate potential risks across its global operations.

In the 1990s, Walmart developed a simplified 5-step ERM framework to assess risk across its vast global operations:

i. Risk Identification:
   1. Senior leaders meet in workshops to identify risks, which are then plotted on a graph of probability vs. impact to prioritize the biggest risks
   2. Risks are categorized into seven areas: legal/regulatory, political, business environment, strategic, operational, financial, and integrity
   3. Risk registers are used to evaluate and determine the priority of risks

ii. Risk Mitigation:
   Operational teams determine if existing procedures effectively address the prioritized risks. Teams that include operational staff in the relevant area meet to address the risks using existing inventory procedures and determine if the procedures are effective

iii. Action Planning:
   A project team identifies and implements next steps over several months to mitigate the prioritized risks

iv. Performance Metrics:
   1. Metrics are developed to measure the impact of the risk mitigation actions
   2. Actual performance is compared to goals over time to assess trends.

v. ROI and Shareholder Value:
   The group assesses the financial impact of the risk mitigation efforts. The impact of the risk mitigation actions on sales and expenses is assessed to determine if shareholder value and ROI have improved.

This structured, data-driven approach allowed Walmart to proactively manage risks and demonstrate value to shareholders.

Walmart's ERM framework is a good example of how a large, complex organization can take a structured approach to managing enterprise-wide risks. By involving senior leadership, operational staff, and using data-driven tools like risk registers and probability/impact graphs, Walmart is able to focus on the most critical risks and implement targeted mitigation strategies.

This case study demonstrates how ERM can be effectively applied in the retail industry to support strategic objectives and create shareholder value.

b. Statoil's ERM Maturity

Statoil, a major Norwegian oil and gas producer, has developed a sophisticated and successful enterprise risk management (ERM) program that is deeply embedded in its business operations. The company's ERM approach focuses on both downside risk and upside potential, recognizing that risk-taking is necessary to create value for shareholders. Statoil's ERM framework is centered on two basic goals: creating value and avoiding accidents. The company aims to thoroughly understand risks, mapping them on probability vs. impact charts that consider both positive and negative outcomes. This contrasts with many ERM programs that are overly focused on regulatory compliance and risk avoidance.

Key elements include:

i. Embedding ERM in the Organization
   1. Risk management is considered a core value at Statoil, integrated into steering documents, corporate policies, and a booklet given to all employees
   2. ERM is thoroughly embedded in the business units' operations and enjoys strong support from executives and the board

ii. Defining Risk Holistically
   1. Statoil defines risk as a deviation from a specified reference value, with associated uncertainties. Risk is measured in terms of impact, probability, and uncertainty factors.
   2. The company recognizes that risk encompasses both downside and upside potential. Risk maps show probability and impact for both negative and positive outcomes.

iii. Aggregating and Coordinating Risk
   1. Statoil has a corporate risk committee that assesses total risk exposure and measures to manage it
   2. The company aims to avoid suboptimal decisions by managing risk from a group perspective and utilizing correlations between risks

iv. Tailoring ERM to the Business
   1. Statoil developed its own ERM framework that made sense for the company, rather than adopting an off-the-shelf solution
   2. The ERM approach is adapted based on the role in the organization, with asset-based entities performing complete risk assessments and delivery entities managing task-specific risks

By deeply embedding ERM in its culture and decision-making, Statoil has been able to make risk management a core part of how it creates value. The company's ERM maturity allows it to take a holistic view of risk and opportunity across the enterprise

Statoil's strong leadership commitment and focus on building a risk-aware culture have been critical to the success of their ERM efforts.

c. Lego: Evolving ERM Over Four Phases

The LEGO Group has successfully evolved its enterprise risk management (ERM) practices over four key phases:

i. Phase 1: Implementing ERM (2006-2007)
   1. In 2006, LEGO's CFO Hans Læssøe introduced ERM to the company, which previously had no formal risk management processes.
   2. Læssøe, with 25 years of LEGO experience, started looking at strategic risk management to address gaps in the ERM portfolio.
   3. By 2007, ERM became a full-time job at LEGO with new positions added in subsequent years.

ii. Phase 2: Monte Carlo Simulations (2008-2009)
   1. LEGO implemented Monte Carlo simulations to help define risk tolerance and evaluate the effect of input variances on complex models.
   2. Simulations were used in three key areas: budget planning, credit risk portfolio, and consolidation of risk exposure.

iii. Phase 3: Active Risk & Opportunity Planning (AROP) (2010-2011)
   1. LEGO developed a formal approach called Active Risk Assessment of Business Projects (AROP) to define and handle project risks.
   2. AROP includes steps for risk identification, assessment, handling, reassessment, follow-up and reporting.

iv. Phase 4: Preparing for Uncertainty (2012-present)
   1. LEGO began preparing for uncertainty by defining and testing strategies through workshops prior to strategic planning.
   2. Four scenarios are developed based on two key drivers of uncertainty, with strategic issues and action plans defined for each.
   3. This "Park, Adapt, Prepare, Act" (PAPA) model allows LEGO to consciously choose strategies to drive value creation.

The evolution of LEGO's ERM practices demonstrates a shift from damage control in the early stages to a more proactive, value-creating approach in later phases. Key success factors include:
1. Aligning ERM with the company's mission, vision and growth/innovation strategies
2. Gaining strong support from upper management
3. Integrating risk management into key planning processes
4. Increasing visibility of enterprise risks to address them more effectively

LEGO's experience shows how ERM can move "upstream" to inform strategic decision making and execution, positioning risk management as a competitive advantage through intelligent risk-taking.

The four-phase approach provides a roadmap for other organizations to evolve their ERM practices to drive conscious strategic choices and create stakeholder value

d. eBay India's Risk Assessment

eBay India conducted a risk assessment to identify and manage risks to its critical business processes and IT systems.

The assessment involved:
i. Identifying threats, vulnerabilities, assets, impact, and likelihood to understand risks. For example, eBay India found that its sales systems were high risk.
ii. Selecting internal controls to reduce the probability of threats or vulnerabilities. This could include measures like temporarily withholding payments from certain sellers until items are delivered on time and in good condition.
iii. Accepting residual risks that remain after controls are implemented, with the goal of supporting eBay's business objectives.

eBay uses the Progress Corticon rules engine to rapidly evaluate thousands of business rules for each transaction and determine if and how much to withhold payment.

This ensures a smooth customer experience by managing risks related to seller performance, item condition, delivery times, and other complex variables.

The risk assessment process allows eBay to proactively identify and mitigate risks to its e-commerce operations. By implementing strong controls and accepting appropriate residual risks, eBay can provide a safe and reliable platform for buyers and sellers while supporting its business goals.

e. Enterprise Risk Management at Intuit

Intuit has implemented a robust Enterprise Risk Management (ERM) program that has evolved over the years to effectively manage risks across the organization. Here are the key aspects of Intuit's ERM approach:

i. Establishing a Common Risk Framework
Intuit established a common risk framework enterprise-wide, enabling business leaders to speak about risks using a common language despite differences in business lines. This framework provides a foundation for consistently identifying, assessing, and managing risks.

ii. Ongoing Risk Assessment
Intuit assesses risks on an ongoing basis, maintaining a constant lens on the risk landscape to increase agility in adapting to changes in the business and operating environment. This regular rhythm of risk management has built a strong risk management capability across the company.

iii. Focus on Significant Risks
Intuit's ERM program focuses attention and resources on the risks with the greatest impact on the company's growth, product delivery, and operations. This targeted approach drives progress in risk mitigation and strengthens risk management capabilities.

iv. Defined Ownership and Accountability
Intuit has clearly defined ownership and accountability for risk management, with business leaders across the company

responsible for managing risks, aligned with their growth strategy and operational priorities. The board and executive management provide appropriate oversight.

v. Performance Measurement and Monitoring

Intuit continuously monitors performance to drive progress in risk mitigation and strengthen risk management capabilities. Key risk indicators (KRIs) are used to understand potential emerging risks and trends that may impact current risks, while key performance indicators (KPIs) help manage current risks.

vi. Cyber Risk Management

Intuit recognizes cyber risk as an enterprise risk and has implemented a cyber risk management toolkit. This toolkit includes elements such as an organization oversight and leadership program, cyber risk assessment, policies, monitoring programs, incident management plans, and cybersecurity awareness education.

By implementing these modern risk management practices, Intuit has built a sustainable ERM program that provides business leaders with an understanding of current and emerging risks, enabling them to make informed strategic decisions. Intuit's ERM journey demonstrates the importance of establishing a common risk framework, assessing risks continuously, focusing on significant risks, defining clear ownership and accountability, and measuring and monitoring performance to effectively manage enterprise-wide risks in today's dynamic business environment.

f. Risk Management Failures at General Motors

General Motors (GM) experienced a major risk management failure in 2014 when it recalled 3.1 million vehicles due to faulty ignition switches that had caused at least 124 deaths. The company had known about the defect for over 10 years but failed to act, demonstrating a fundamental breakdown in its enterprise risk management (ERM) program.

GM's risk management failure highlights several key lessons for modern businesses:

i. Risk management must be more than just a process.
Having an ERM program on paper is not enough - the company must have a genuine risk management culture that prioritizes identifying, assessing and mitigating risks at all levels. GM's ERM system failed to prevent or even detect the ignition switch issue for many years.

ii. Risks must be owned and managed proactively.
No one at GM seemed to take responsibility for the ignition switch risk, so no mitigation plans were developed. Risks can't be ignored just because they seem low probability - companies must anticipate and prepare for them.

iii. Communication and feedback loops are critical.
The ignition switch defect was not communicated up the chain for a decade. Effective ERM requires open reporting of risks and a continuous feedback loop to evaluate and adjust risk management strategies.

iv. Operational failures, not just financial risks, must be managed.
Operational risks like product defects can have catastrophic consequences, even for a large company like GM. Focusing only on financial risks is not enough.

v. Tone at the top matters.
GM's leadership, including the CEO, touted the company's ERM program but failed to ensure it was actually working. Effective risk management requires commitment and accountability from the top.

In the aftermath of the recall crisis, GM made changes to its risk management approach, including appointing a Global Vehicle Safety Chief.

However, the company's failure to identify and address the ignition switch issue for so long demonstrates the need for a more proactive, comprehensive approach to risk management in modern business.

g. Risk Management Failures at Toyota

Toyota has faced several risk management failures in recent years that have significantly impacted its operations and reputation. Here are some key issues and lessons for modern risk management in business:

i. Design Flaws and Quality Issues
Toyota had to recall over 9 million vehicles worldwide due to issues with unintended acceleration caused by design flaws in the accelerator pedal and floor mat systems. These quality problems posed serious safety risks, resulted in accidents and fatalities, and severely damaged Toyota's reputation for reliability. Effective risk management requires proactively identifying and mitigating product design and quality risks before issues arise.

ii. Supplier Disruptions
In 2022, a cyberattack on a key supplier forced Toyota to halt production at all 28 lines in 14 Japanese plants for a day. This demonstrates the domino effect that supplier failures can have on a company's operations. Robust risk management involves assessing the security and resilience of critical suppliers, monitoring for threats, and having incident response plans to quickly mitigate supplier disruptions.

iii. Weak Management and Communication
Toyota's recall crisis was partly attributed to weak management strategies and poor communication between departments. Effective risk management requires strong leadership, clear communication channels, and alignment across the organization to identify and address risks. Siloed departments and lack of coordination can lead to issues being overlooked.

iv. Overconfidence and Complacency
Toyota's success and position as the world's largest automaker may have bred overconfidence and complacency, leading it to neglect public relations and risk management efforts. Even market leaders are susceptible to risks. Effective risk management requires constant vigilance, humility, and a willingness to invest in risk mitigation, even when times are good.

v. Lack of Catastrophe Planning
Toyota was caught off guard by the 2011 earthquake and tsunami in Japan, which disrupted its supply chain and production despite its plants being relatively undamaged. Comprehensive risk management must consider low-probability, high-impact events and have contingency plans to maintain operations. Relying solely on past history is insufficient.

In summary, Toyota's risk management failures highlight the need for modern businesses to proactively identify and mitigate a wide range of risks, from product design to supplier disruptions to natural disasters. Strong leadership, communication, supplier due diligence, and catastrophe planning are critical to building resilient organizations that can withstand unexpected challenges.

h. Lululemon's Yoga Pants Recall

In March 2013, Lululemon faced a major crisis when it had to recall 17% of its women's black yoga pants due to the fabric being too sheer, meaning the pants became semi-see through when bent at certain angles. This recall, which cost the company an estimated $67 million, highlighted several key lessons about modern risk management in business:

i. Clearly articulate risks:
    Lululemon's risk descriptions in their 10-K filings were too vague and grouped multiple risks together, making it difficult to assess the impact and likelihood of each risk. Risks should be listed as specific events to enable better risk assessment and treatment.

ii. Enhance product testing:
    Lululemon acknowledged that while the recalled pants met testing standards, the fabric was on the low end of their tolerance scale. More comprehensive testing protocols are needed to catch quality issues before products reach consumers.

iii. Develop a robust recall plan:
    Companies must have a complete plan of action for recalls, considering not just the immediate actions but also the potential ramifications in the weeks following. Lululemon faced a PR disaster and the departure of its Chief Product Officer due to the recall.

iv. Manage social media risk:
    The recall quickly turned into a full-blown crisis as outraged customers took to social media. Companies need to monitor social media and have a strategy to respond to reputational risks in real-time.

v. Make risk a board-level priority:
The Lululemon case shows that risk-related matters can quickly become a board-level issue, from the financial impact to the reputational damage and executive departures. Boards must be actively engaged in overseeing risk management.

By learning from Lululemon's experience, companies can enhance their risk management practices to better identify, assess, and respond to risks in today's fast-paced, socially connected business environment.

i. Crowdsourcing to Reduce Movie-Making Risk

Crowdsourcing can help reduce the risk of movie-making by tapping into the collective wisdom of the crowd to make more informed decisions about projects. Unlike other industries where risks can be tested along the way, each movie is a huge financial investment with a high degree of uncertainty. Crowdsourcing allows studios to gather insights from a large number of people on what ideas seem most promising before committing millions of dollars.

Some ways crowdsourcing is being used in the movie industry include:

i. The Black List, an annual compilation of promising scripts recommended by anonymous Hollywood insiders
ii. Platforms like KinoLime that let fans crowdsource every stage of the filmmaking process, from funding to production
iii. Models like HeroX that allow filmmakers to post production tasks that freelancers can bid on.

Crowdsourcing provides valuable data to help determine the best course of action and avoid costly flops. It enables studios to make more informed decisions based on the collective input of the crowd rather than relying solely on the gut instinct of individual producers.

However, crowdsourcing the entire movie-making process from start to finish is still very challenging. The key value propositions of crowdsourcing - modularity, customer selection, and talent aggregation - are not as applicable to the creative and collaborative nature of filmmaking.

Crafting a script or filming a movie by committee is almost always destined to fail.

That said, crowdsourcing can still play a valuable role in reducing risk by gathering audience feedback during the pre-screening and editing process. While not true crowdsourcing, this allows studios to incorporate consumer insights before finalizing the film.

In summary, while crowdsourcing the entire movie-making process is not realistic, it can be a powerful tool for studios to gather data, validate ideas, and make more informed decisions to reduce the inherent risks of big-budget filmmaking. Combining the wisdom of the crowd with the expertise of industry professionals is a promising approach for the future of the movie business.

j. Integrating Technology and Data Analytics

Many companies are leveraging advanced technologies like AI, machine learning and big data analytics to enhance their risk management capabilities:
1. AI and machine learning enable real-time risk monitoring and prediction by analyzing vast amounts of data
2. Big data analytics provide deeper insights by uncovering patterns and trends in historical and real-time information
3. Automation streamlines risk assessment and mitigation processes

Integrating these technologies into ERM allows companies to identify emerging risks faster, make more informed decisions, and respond proactively.

In summary, leading companies are taking a strategic, data-driven approach to ERM that involves senior leadership, a structured framework, employee engagement, continuous improvement, and leveraging the latest technologies.

By proactively managing risks, organizations can safeguard their assets, reputation and shareholder value.

15 BEST PRACTICES

As we recall, risk management is a critical process for identifying, assessing, and mitigating potential threats to a business.

In today's rapidly changing business environment, organizations must take a proactive and strategic approach to risk management to ensure their long-term success and resilience.

Here are some best practices for modern risk management in business:

a. Conduct Regular Risk Assessments
Conducting regular risk assessments is a critical best practice in modern risk management for businesses.

This practice involves systematically identifying, analyzing, and evaluating potential risks that could impact an organization's operations, objectives, or assets.

Regular risk assessments help businesses stay ahead of potential threats and vulnerabilities by keeping their risk profile up to date. This ensures that business leaders have the most current information available when making decisions that could affect the organization's risk exposure.

The frequency of risk assessments can vary depending on the organization's needs and industry requirements. Some businesses conduct assessments annually, while others may do so quarterly or even monthly. The key is to establish a consistent schedule that allows for timely identification and mitigation of new or evolving risks.

When conducting risk assessments, organizations should follow a structured process:

i. Define the scope of the assessment
ii. Identify potential risks from various sources, including operational, financial, compliance, and reputational risks
iii. Analyze and evaluate the identified risks
iv. Develop risk treatment plans
v. Implement controls and mitigation strategies
vi. Monitor and review the effectiveness of risk management efforts

Regular risk assessments offer several benefits to businesses:
i. Proactive risk management: By identifying potential threats early, organizations can take preventive measures before issues escalate.
ii. Improved decision-making: Up-to-date risk information enables leaders to make more informed choices about resource allocation and strategic planning.
iii. Enhanced compliance: Many industries have regulatory requirements for risk management, and regular assessments help ensure compliance.
iv. Increased operational efficiency: Identifying and addressing risks can lead to process improvements and reduced vulnerabilities.
v. Better stakeholder communication: Regular assessments provide valuable data for reporting to stakeholders, including investors, regulators, and employees.

To maximize the effectiveness of regular risk assessments, organizations should:
i. Involve diverse stakeholders from across the business to gain comprehensive insights.
ii. Utilize technology tools and solutions to streamline the assessment process and improve accuracy.
iii. Foster a risk-aware culture where employees at all levels understand the importance of identifying and reporting potential risks.
iv. Continuously improve the assessment process based on lessons learned and changes in the business environment.

By making regular risk assessments a cornerstone of their risk management strategy, businesses can better protect themselves against potential threats, seize opportunities, and maintain a competitive edge in today's dynamic business landscape.

b. Quantify and Prioritize Risks
Quantifying and prioritizing risks is a crucial best practice in modern risk management for businesses. This approach allows organizations to systematically evaluate and rank potential threats, enabling more effective allocation of resources and development of targeted mitigation strategies.

The process of quantifying risks involves assigning numerical values to the likelihood and potential impact of identified risks. This quantification can be achieved through various methods, including:
 i. Predictive analytics: Using historical data and advanced algorithms to forecast potential risks and their probabilities.
 ii. Scenario analysis: Evaluating different possible outcomes and their consequences to assess risk severity.
 iii. Monte Carlo simulations: Running multiple simulations to model various risk scenarios and their potential impacts.

By quantifying risks, businesses can move beyond subjective assessments and make data-driven decisions about which risks require immediate attention and resources.

Once risks are quantified, the next step is prioritization. This involves ranking risks based on their potential impact and likelihood of occurrence. Prioritization helps organizations to:
 i. Focus on critical risks: Identify and address the most significant threats to the business first.
 ii. Allocate resources efficiently: Direct time, money, and personnel to the areas of highest risk.
 iii. Develop targeted strategies: Create specific mitigation plans for high-priority risks.

Key Risk Indicators (KRIs) play a vital role in this process, serving as measurable metrics that indicate the level of exposure to a particular risk. By regularly monitoring and updating these KRIs, businesses can maintain an up-to-date understanding of their risk landscape and adjust their strategies accordingly.

The benefits of quantifying and prioritizing risks extend beyond immediate risk mitigation. This approach also:
i. Enhances decision-making: Provides a clear, data-driven basis for strategic choices.
ii. Improves resource allocation: Ensures that risk management efforts are focused where they're most needed.
iii. Facilitates communication: Offers a standardized way to discuss and report on risks across the organization.
iv. Supports compliance: Helps in meeting regulatory requirements by demonstrating a systematic approach to risk management.

To implement this best practice effectively, organizations should:
i. Use a combination of qualitative and quantitative methods for a comprehensive risk assessment.
ii. Regularly review and update risk assessments to reflect changes in the business environment.
iii. Involve stakeholders from various departments to ensure a holistic view of potential risks.
iv. Leverage technology and advanced tools to automate and streamline the quantification and prioritization process.

By adopting the practice of quantifying and prioritizing risks, businesses can create a more robust and responsive risk management framework. This approach not only helps in mitigating potential threats but also positions the organization to capitalize on opportunities that arise from well-managed risks, ultimately contributing to long-term success and resilience.

c. Implement Risk Mitigation Measures
Implementing risk mitigation measures is a crucial step in modern risk management for businesses. This practice involves executing strategies and actions designed to reduce the likelihood or impact of identified risks.

Risk mitigation measures are typically implemented after a thorough risk assessment has been conducted and potential threats have been identified. These measures are proactive steps taken to address vulnerabilities and protect the organization from potential harm.

Key aspects of implementing risk mitigation measures include:
i. Prioritization: Focus on addressing the most critical risks first, based on their potential impact and likelihood of occurrence.
ii. Tailored strategies: Develop and implement specific measures for each identified risk. These may include:
 1) Implementing internal controls
 2) Diversifying business operations
 3) Investing in technology and cybersecurity
 4) Establishing contingency plans
iii. Security controls: Deploy technical safeguards such as firewalls, encryption, and access controls to protect against digital threats.
iv. Training and awareness: Educate employees about risk management practices and their role in maintaining security. This helps foster a risk-aware culture within the organization.
v. Continuous monitoring: Regularly review and assess the effectiveness of implemented measures, adjusting them as needed to address evolving risks.
vi. Documentation: Develop and maintain clear risk mitigation plans that outline specific risk reduction steps. These plans should be shared with all relevant team members.
vii. Compliance: Ensure that risk mitigation measures align with relevant legal and regulatory requirements.
viii. Collaboration: Work closely with stakeholders, including IT departments, security teams, and management, to implement comprehensive risk mitigation strategies.

By implementing robust risk mitigation measures, businesses can:
Reduce the likelihood of adverse events occurring
i. Minimize the potential impact of risks that do materialize
ii. Improve overall organizational resilience
iii. Enhance decision-making processes
iv. Protect valuable assets and resources
v. Maintain business continuity in the face of challenges

It's important to note that risk mitigation is an ongoing process. As the business environment evolves and new threats emerge, organizations must continually reassess their risk landscape and adjust their mitigation measures accordingly. This adaptive approach ensures that the business remains protected against current and future risks, supporting long-term sustainability and success.

d. Foster a Risk-Aware Culture

Fostering a risk-aware culture is a critical best practice for modern risk management in business. This approach ensures that risk management is integrated into the daily operations and decision-making processes of an organization, promoting resilience and long-term success.

Here are key strategies to foster a risk-aware culture:

　　i. Leadership Commitment

　　　Leadership plays a pivotal role in establishing and maintaining a risk-aware culture. Leaders must exemplify risk-aware decision-making and prioritize risk management in strategic discussions. Their commitment sets the tone for the entire organization, encouraging employees to follow suit.

　　ii. Continuous Education and Training

　　　Ongoing education and training are essential to ensure that employees at all levels understand the risks inherent in their activities. This can include workshops, seminars, and simulated scenarios to help employees recognize and manage risks effectively.

　　iii. Open Communication Channels

　　　Creating an environment where employees can report risks and concerns without fear of retribution is crucial. Open communication channels encourage transparency and allow for the early identification and mitigation of potential risks.

　　iv. Incentivizing Risk-Aware Behavior

　　　Aligning reward systems with risk management objectives can motivate employees to prioritize risk awareness. For example, offering bonuses for developing secure software or recognizing teams that effectively manage risks can reinforce the desired behaviors.

　　v. Regular Risk Assessments

　　　Conducting regular risk assessments helps identify new risks and reassess existing ones. This proactive approach ensures that the organization remains vigilant and prepared

to address potential threats.
vi. Integrating Risk Management into Innovation
Balancing risk management with innovation is essential. Integrating risk evaluation into the innovation process, such as using stage-gate processes, allows for the identification and mitigation of risks early on. This approach supports creativity while managing potential downsides.
vii. Cross-Functional Risk Committees
Establishing cross-functional risk committees ensures a holistic view of risks across the organization. These committees can include members from various departments, such as finance, operations, and legal, to provide diverse perspectives on risk management.
viii. Leveraging Technology
Utilizing advanced analytics and AI can provide deeper insights into risk patterns and enhance the organization's ability to detect and respond to risks. Technology can also streamline risk assessment, monitoring, and reporting processes.
ix. Aligning Risk Culture with Organizational Values
A risk-aware culture must align with the organization's core values and business objectives. Integrating risk management into the organization's vision and mission statements reinforces its importance and ensures that it is a fundamental part of the business strategy.
x. Leadership and Governance
Effective governance structures, such as risk committees and clear policies, support a risk-aware culture. Leaders must model risk-aware behaviors and make decisions that reflect a commitment to managing risks responsibly.

By fostering a risk-aware culture, organizations can navigate uncertainties more effectively, enhance resilience, and support long-term success. This culture empowers employees to proactively manage risks, contributing to the overall stability and growth of the organization.

e. Develop a Comprehensive Risk Management Plan
Developing a comprehensive risk management plan is a critical

best practice for modern businesses to effectively identify, assess, and mitigate potential threats to their operations. This proactive approach helps organizations safeguard their assets, reputation, and long-term success.

A comprehensive risk management plan begins with thorough risk identification and prioritization. This involves systematically assessing the likelihood and potential impact of various risks on the business. By identifying and prioritizing risks, companies can allocate resources more effectively and develop targeted mitigation strategies.

Once risks are identified, the next step is to create a detailed risk mitigation plan. This plan should outline specific actions and measures to reduce the impact of identified risks. It's crucial to involve key stakeholders in the planning process to ensure the plan is comprehensive and tailored to the organization's unique needs.

A well-structured risk management plan typically includes the following components:
i. Risk identification and analysis
ii. Risk response strategies
iii. Risk monitoring and control mechanisms

The plan should clearly document all identified risks, their potential impact, and the likelihood of occurrence. It should also define specific strategies for addressing each risk, which may include risk avoidance, transfer, mitigation, or acceptance.

Implementing the risk management plan is an ongoing process that requires regular monitoring and evaluation. By consistently reviewing the effectiveness of risk mitigation strategies, businesses can identify emerging risks or areas for improvement. This allows for timely adjustments to maintain the plan's effectiveness.

Communication and collaboration are essential elements of a successful risk management plan. Ensuring that all stakeholders are aware of the risks facing the business and their role in mitigating them promotes a culture of risk awareness throughout the organization. Regular communication and collaboration among teams can help identify and address risks more efficiently.

Employee training and education play a crucial role in the success of a risk management plan. Providing comprehensive training on risk management principles and practices empowers employees to identify and respond to risks effectively. Regular training sessions reinforce best practices and help maintain a risk-aware culture within the organization.

Finally, fostering a culture of continuous improvement is vital for long-term risk management success. Encouraging employees to report potential risks or suggest improvements helps organizations stay ahead of emerging threats. By continuously striving for improvement, businesses can adapt their risk management strategies to evolving challenges and maintain their competitive edge.

In conclusion, developing a comprehensive risk management plan is an essential best practice for modern businesses. By systematically identifying, assessing, and mitigating risks, organizations can protect their assets, reputation, and long-term success in an increasingly complex and uncertain business environment.

f. Regularly Review and Update Strategies
    Regularly reviewing and updating strategies is a critical best practice for modern risk management in business. This approach ensures that risk mitigation strategies remain effective and aligned with the evolving business environment, emerging risks, and lessons learned from past experiences. Here are key aspects of this practice:
    i. Adaptation to Changing Environments
        Risk landscapes are dynamic, influenced by factors such as market conditions, technological advancements, regulatory changes, and geopolitical events. Regularly reviewing and updating strategies allows businesses to adapt to these changes proactively. This involves conducting periodic risk assessments, monitoring industry trends, and seeking feedback from stakeholders to ensure

that risk mitigation measures are current and relevant.
ii. Continuous Monitoring and Feedback
Continuous monitoring of risk indicators and early warning systems is essential for detecting emerging risks. By regularly assessing the impact of implemented controls and identifying new threats, businesses can make necessary adjustments to their strategies. This proactive approach helps in maintaining the effectiveness of risk mitigation efforts and ensures that the organization is prepared for potential disruptions.
iii. Learning from Past Experiences
Analyzing past incidents and near-misses provides valuable insights for refining risk mitigation strategies. By identifying patterns or recurring issues, businesses can incorporate lessons learned into their future risk response plans. This iterative process of learning and improvement enhances the organization's resilience and ability to manage risks effectively.
iv. Stakeholder Involvement
Engaging stakeholders in the review and update process ensures that diverse perspectives are considered, and that the strategies are comprehensive. This can involve collaboration with Managed Service Providers (MSPs), employees, and other key partners to align risk management efforts with overall business objectives. Regular communication and reporting help in maintaining alignment and fostering a culture of continuous improvement.
v. Strategic Alignment
Regularly updating risk management strategies ensures that they remain aligned with the organization's strategic goals. This involves integrating risk management into strategic planning sessions, defining key performance indicators (KPIs), and developing a strategic IT roadmap that supports business objectives. By doing so, businesses can ensure that their risk mitigation efforts contribute directly to achieving their long-term goals.

In summary, regularly reviewing and updating risk management strategies is essential for maintaining their effectiveness in a constantly changing environment. This practice involves continuous monitoring, learning from past experiences, engaging stakeholders, and aligning strategies with business objectives. By adopting this approach, businesses can enhance their resilience, protect their reputation, and achieve sustainable growth.

g. Engage All Stakeholders
Engaging all stakeholders is a critical best practice in modern risk management for businesses. This approach ensures that all potential impacts are considered and addressed, leading to more comprehensive and effective risk management strategies. Here are the key aspects of this practice:
   i. Comprehensive Risk Identification
      Engaging all stakeholders in the risk management process allows for a more thorough identification of risks. Stakeholders, including employees, customers, suppliers, and community members, can provide diverse perspectives and insights into potential risks that might not be apparent to the management alone. This holistic approach ensures that no significant risk is overlooked.
   ii. Improved Communication and Collaboration
      Effective stakeholder engagement fosters better communication and collaboration. By involving stakeholders in the risk management process, businesses can ensure that everyone is on the same page regarding potential risks and the strategies to mitigate them. This collaborative environment helps in building trust and ensures that stakeholders are more likely to support and adhere to risk management plans.
   iii. Enhanced Decision-Making
      When all stakeholders are engaged, decision-making processes benefit from a wider range of inputs and perspectives. This diversity in viewpoints can lead to more innovative and effective solutions to manage risks. Additionally, it helps in aligning the risk management strategies with the values and expectations of all stakeholders, which is crucial for long-term success.
   iv. Increased Accountability and Transparency
      Engaging stakeholders increases accountability and transparency in the risk management process. Stakeholders

are more likely to hold the organization accountable for its risk management practices when they are actively involved. This transparency can enhance the organization's reputation and build stronger relationships with stakeholders.

v. Better Risk Mitigation
By considering the insights and concerns of all stakeholders, businesses can develop more robust risk mitigation strategies. Stakeholders can provide valuable information about potential vulnerabilities and suggest practical measures to address them. This comprehensive approach to risk mitigation can significantly reduce the likelihood and impact of risks.

vi. Long-Term Sustainability
Engaging all stakeholders aligns with the principles of sustainable business practices. It ensures that the company's risk management strategies consider not only financial outcomes but also the social and environmental impacts. This alignment with broader sustainability goals can enhance the company's reputation and contribute to its long-term success.

In conclusion, engaging all stakeholders in the risk management process is a best practice that leads to more comprehensive risk identification, improved communication, enhanced decision-making, increased accountability, better risk mitigation, and long-term sustainability. This holistic approach is essential for modern businesses aiming to navigate the complex and dynamic risk landscape effectively.

h. Leverage Technology
Leveraging technology is a crucial best practice for modern risk management in business. By harnessing the power of advanced tools and systems, organizations can significantly enhance their ability to identify, assess, monitor, and mitigate risks more effectively and efficiently.

One of the primary benefits of leveraging technology in risk management is the ability to process and analyze vast amounts of data in real-time. This capability allows businesses to detect patterns, anomalies, and trends that may indicate emerging or evolving risks. For example, artificial intelligence (AI) and machine learning (ML) algorithms can be employed to identify potential risks that human analysts might overlook, providing a more comprehensive risk assessment.

Real-time monitoring is another key advantage of technology-driven risk management. Advanced systems can continuously track risk indicators and trigger instant alerts when predefined thresholds are breached. This enables risk managers to respond promptly to potential threats, minimizing their impact on the organization. For instance, an automated system can notify relevant personnel immediately if a company's stock price drops below a certain level, prompting swift investigation and action.

Technology also facilitates more sophisticated risk analysis through scenario modeling and simulation. These tools allow risk managers to test various "what-if" scenarios and assess their potential impact on the organization. By simulating different risk events and outcomes, businesses can better prepare for a range of possibilities and develop more robust risk mitigation strategies.

Integration of risk management systems with other business processes is another critical aspect of leveraging technology. By connecting risk management tools with existing systems, organizations can gain a holistic view of their risk landscape across different departments and functions. This integration enables more informed decision-making and a more coordinated approach to risk management.

Automation is a key feature of technology-driven risk management. By automating routine tasks such as data collection, analysis, and reporting, businesses can save time and reduce the potential for human error. This allows risk managers to focus on more strategic activities, such as developing risk mitigation strategies and communicating with stakeholders.

Advanced analytics and predictive modeling are powerful tools in modern risk management. These technologies enable businesses to anticipate potential risks and their impacts more accurately. By leveraging historical data and current trends, predictive analytics can help organizations stay ahead of emerging risks and take proactive measures to address them.

Lastly, technology plays a crucial role in enhancing communication and collaboration in risk management. Cloud-based platforms and collaborative tools allow risk managers to share information, coordinate responses, and engage stakeholders more effectively. This improved communication ensures that all relevant parties are informed and aligned in their approach to risk management.

In conclusion, leveraging technology is essential for modern risk management in business. By embracing advanced tools and systems, organizations can significantly improve their ability to identify, assess, and mitigate risks, ultimately enhancing their resilience and competitiveness in today's dynamic business environment.

i. Leverage Existing Frameworks and Best Practices
Leveraging existing frameworks and best practices is a crucial strategy for modern risk management in business. This approach allows organizations to build upon established methodologies and industry standards, saving time and resources while ensuring a comprehensive and effective risk management process.
One of the primary advantages of leveraging existing frameworks is the access to proven methodologies. Organizations can benefit from widely recognized standards such as ISO 31000, NIST Risk Management Framework (RMF), and COSO Enterprise Risk Management (ERM). These frameworks provide structured approaches to identifying, assessing, and mitigating risks, offering a solid foundation for organizations to build their risk management practices upon.

By adopting established frameworks, businesses can ensure they are aligning with industry best practices. This alignment not only enhances the effectiveness of risk management efforts but also demonstrates due diligence to stakeholders, regulators, and partners. It shows that the organization is committed to following recognized standards in managing risks, which can be particularly important in regulated industries or when dealing with sensitive information.

Existing frameworks often come with pre-existing risk assessment templates and tools, such as the Factor Analysis of Information Risk (FAIR) methodology. These resources can significantly streamline the risk assessment process, providing a structured approach to quantifying risks and prioritizing mitigation efforts. This can be especially valuable for organizations that may not have extensive in-house risk management expertise.

Another benefit of leveraging existing frameworks is the ability to benchmark against industry peers. Many of these frameworks are widely adopted across various sectors, allowing organizations to compare their risk management practices and performance with others in their industry. This benchmarking can help identify areas for improvement and validate the effectiveness of current risk management strategies.

It's important to note that while leveraging existing frameworks is beneficial, organizations should adapt these frameworks to fit their specific needs and risk profile. No two businesses are identical, and risk management practices should be tailored to address the unique challenges and objectives of each organization.
Continuous improvement is also a key aspect of leveraging existing frameworks. As new threats emerge and business environments evolve, organizations should regularly review and update their risk management practices. Many established frameworks are periodically updated to address new risks and incorporate lessons learned, providing a valuable resource for organizations to stay current with best practices.

In conclusion, leveraging existing frameworks and best practices is a smart approach to modern risk management. It provides a solid foundation, ensures alignment with industry standards, offers valuable tools and resources, enables benchmarking, and supports continuous improvement. By adopting this strategy, businesses can enhance their risk management capabilities and better protect themselves against potential threats and uncertainties.

j. Implement Minimum Viable Product (MVP) Development
Implementing Minimum Viable Product (MVP) development is a crucial best practice for modern risk management in business. This approach allows companies to validate their ideas, minimize potential losses, and iterate quickly based on user feedback.

An MVP is a version of a product with just enough features to satisfy early customers and provide feedback for future development. The primary goal is to test fundamental business hypotheses and gather insights with minimal investment of time and resources.

Here's why MVP development is essential for risk management:
   i. Reduced financial risk:
      By focusing on core functionality, companies can minimize initial development costs and avoid investing heavily in unproven concepts.
   ii. Faster time-to-market:
      MVPs can be launched quickly, allowing businesses to gain a competitive advantage and start generating revenue sooner.
   iii. Early user feedback:
      Releasing an MVP enables companies to gather real-world user data and validate their assumptions about market needs.
   iv. Iterative improvement:
      The MVP approach allows for continuous refinement based on user feedback, ensuring that subsequent versions better align with customer expectations.
   v. Flexibility and adaptability:
      If the initial concept proves unsuccessful, businesses can pivot or make necessary changes with minimal sunk costs.
   vi. Improved resource allocation:
      By focusing on essential features, companies can allocate resources more efficiently and avoid wasting time on unnecessary elements.
   vii. Enhanced investor appeal:
      A working MVP can demonstrate a product's potential to investors, increasing the likelihood of securing funding.

To implement MVP development effectively:
   i. Identify core features:
      Determine the essential functionalities that address the primary user problem.
   ii. Prioritize stability:
      Minimize the use of external plugins and libraries to reduce potential risks and ensure a stable product.
   iii. Conduct thorough planning:
      Implement efficient code with careful planning to mitigate potential risks.
   iv. Utilize agile methodologies:
      Employ iterative development processes to facilitate rapid product delivery and adaptation.
   v. Continuous testing and feedback:
      Regularly test the MVP and incorporate user feedback to improve performance and meet user needs.
   vi. Set clear performance metrics:
      Establish key performance indicators (KPIs) to measure the MVP's success and guide future development.

By adopting MVP development as a risk management strategy, businesses can validate their ideas, minimize potential losses, and make data-driven decisions about future product development. This approach allows companies to remain agile in rapidly changing markets and reduce the likelihood of investing significant resources in products that may not meet customer needs or expectations.

k. Conduct Contingency Planning
Conducting contingency planning is a critical component of modern risk management in business. It involves developing strategies and procedures to respond effectively to potential disruptions or crises that could impact an organization's operations.

Contingency planning is a proactive process that analyzes specific potential events or situations that may pose risks to the business. The goal is to establish response arrangements in advance, enabling the organization to react quickly and effectively when faced with unexpected challenges.

Key aspects of effective contingency planning include:
i. Risk assessment: Identify and analyze potential risks and threats to the organization.
ii. Scenario development: Create multiple scenarios, including worst-case situations, to plan for various potential outcomes.
iii. Resource allocation: Ensure the availability of necessary resources, including personnel, equipment, and funding, to implement the plan when needed.
iv. Clear responsibilities: Assign specific roles and responsibilities to team members for executing the plan.
v. Flexibility: Design plans that are adaptable to changing circumstances and can be adjusted as needed.
vi. Regular updates: Review and revise the plan annually or more frequently to keep it current and relevant.
vii. Testing and exercises: Conduct regular drills or simulations to test the effectiveness of the plan and identify areas for improvement.
viii. Communication protocols: Establish clear communication channels and procedures for coordinating responses during a crisis.

The benefits of robust contingency planning include:
i. Protection of lives and property: Minimizing the impact of potential disasters or disruptions.
ii. Enhanced coordination: Improving collaboration between different departments and stakeholders during crisis situations.
iii. Compliance: Meeting regulatory requirements and industry standards for risk management.
iv. Business continuity: Ensuring the organization can maintain or quickly resume critical operations during and after a disruption.
v. Reputation management: Demonstrating preparedness and responsibility to stakeholders, customers, and the public.

In today's complex and interconnected business environment, contingency planning is essential for organizations of all sizes and industries. It helps businesses anticipate potential challenges, minimize their impact, and recover more quickly from disruptions. By investing time and resources in comprehensive contingency planning, companies can build resilience and maintain a competitive edge in the face of uncertainty.

1. **Perform Root Cause Analysis and Document Lessons Learned**
   Performing root cause analysis (RCA) and documenting lessons learned are critical best practices for modern risk management in business. These processes help organizations identify the underlying causes of incidents, prevent future occurrences, and continuously improve their risk management strategies.

   Root cause analysis is a systematic approach to investigating and identifying the fundamental reasons behind an incident or problem. It goes beyond addressing surface-level symptoms to uncover the deeper issues that enabled or facilitated the event. The primary goal of RCA is to answer key questions about what happened, how it happened, why it happened, and how it can be prevented or mitigated in the future.

   To conduct an effective RCA, organizations should:
   i. Gather and analyze relevant data, including logs, alerts, reports, and forensic evidence.
   ii. Use various tools and techniques such as timeline analysis, network traffic analysis, and event correlation.
   iii. Apply structured frameworks like the fishbone diagram, the 5 whys, or fault tree analysis to guide the process.
   iv. Involve relevant stakeholders and participants throughout the analysis.
   v. Focus on facts and solutions rather than blame and faults.

   Documenting lessons learned is an equally important part of the process. This involves evaluating and improving incident response and recovery performance.

   A lesson learned review (LLR) should:
   i. Gather input from all stakeholders involved in the incident.
   ii. Review and update incident response plans, policies, and procedures.
   iii. Identify strengths and weaknesses in the organization's

      response capabilities.
iv. Use tools like surveys, interviews, SWOT analysis, or after-action reports to support the review.

The benefits of conducting RCA and documenting lessons learned include:
i. Reducing the likelihood and impact of future incidents by addressing root causes.
ii. Improving the efficiency and effectiveness of incident response and recovery processes.
iii. Enhancing overall network security awareness and culture within the organization.
iv. Demonstrating compliance and accountability by documenting and reporting results.

To maximize the benefits of these practices, organizations should:
i. Plan ahead and prepare for the process by defining roles, responsibilities, and tools.
ii. Engage stakeholders throughout the entire process.
iii. Maintain a constructive and positive attitude focused on improvement.
iv. Follow up and monitor progress on action items and outcomes.
v. Apply the lessons learned to improve future performance and risk management strategies.

It's important to note that RCA and lessons learned reviews should not be limited to failures or negative events. Organizations can also learn valuable lessons from successes and unexpected positive outcomes. By consistently applying these practices to both positive and negative events, businesses can create a culture of continuous improvement and more effectively manage risks in their operations.

In conclusion, performing root cause analysis and documenting lessons learned are essential components of modern risk management. These practices enable organizations to learn from past experiences, address underlying issues, and continuously improve their risk management strategies, ultimately leading to more resilient and successful businesses.

m. Stay Informed About Risks and Trends
Staying informed about risks and trends is a critical best practice for modern risk management in business. This approach enables organizations to anticipate potential threats, adapt to changing environments, and make informed decisions to protect their interests.

To effectively stay informed, risk managers should employ a multi-faceted approach:
   i. Leverage risk intelligence platforms: These tools aggregate and analyze data from various sources to provide real-time insights into emerging risks and industry developments. By utilizing such platforms, risk managers can quickly identify potential threats and opportunities, allowing for proactive decision-making.
   ii. Engage in continuous learning: Attend conferences, webinars, and workshops focused on risk management topics. These events offer opportunities to learn about the latest trends, best practices, and emerging challenges in the field. Additionally, they provide valuable networking opportunities with other professionals, fostering knowledge exchange and collaboration.
   iii. Monitor industry publications and research: Regularly read reputable publications, research papers, and reports related to risk management and your specific industry. This practice helps you stay abreast of the latest developments, regulatory changes, and emerging risks that may impact your organization.
   iv. Utilize data analytics: Implement advanced analytics tools to process and interpret large volumes of data related to your organization's risk landscape. These tools can help identify patterns, trends, and potential risks that may not be immediately apparent through traditional analysis methods.
   v. Engage with stakeholders: Regularly consult with department heads, subject matter experts, and frontline employees to gather information about potential risks and mitigation strategies. This approach ensures that you have a comprehensive understanding of risks across all levels of the organization.

vi. Participate in industry associations and forums: Join relevant industry groups and participate in discussions and forums focused on risk management. These platforms provide opportunities to share experiences, learn from peers, and stay informed about industry-specific risks and trends.

vii. Conduct regular risk assessments: Perform thorough and frequent risk assessments to identify new and evolving risks within your organization. This practice helps ensure that your risk management strategies remain current and effective.

viii. Establish a risk-aware culture: Foster an environment where employees at all levels are encouraged to report potential risks and share insights. This collective approach to risk identification can help uncover emerging threats that may not be visible at the management level.

By implementing these practices, modern risk managers can create a robust system for staying informed about risks and trends. This proactive approach enables organizations to anticipate challenges, seize opportunities, and maintain a competitive edge in an increasingly complex business environment.

n. Communicate Effectively
Effective communication is a cornerstone of modern risk management in business. It ensures that all stakeholders are informed, engaged, and aligned in their understanding and approach to managing risks.

Effective communication is essential for identifying, evaluating, and managing risks within an organization. It allows stakeholders to share information, ideas, and concerns, ensuring that everyone understands their role in the risk management process. Without clear communication, risks can go unnoticed or unaddressed, potentially leading to significant harm to the organization.

Here are some best practices for communicating effectively in risk management:

i. Establish Clear Communication Channels
Organizations should set up clear communication channels and protocols to ensure that risk-related information flows smoothly among all stakeholders. This includes using various communication tools such as emails, meetings, and digital platforms to keep everyone informed.

ii. Develop a Common Language
Creating a common language for discussing risks helps in reducing misunderstandings and ensures that all stakeholders are on the same page. This involves using plain language and avoiding technical jargon that might confuse non-experts.

iii. Foster Open Communication
Encouraging open and transparent communication across all levels of the organization is crucial. This includes sharing risk-related information, concerns, and insights among employees, management, and other stakeholders. Open communication helps in identifying risks early and developing effective mitigation strategies.

iv. Involve Stakeholders
Involving relevant stakeholders in the risk management process fosters collaboration and shared accountability. Stakeholders, including employees, management, customers, suppliers, and regulatory bodies, bring diverse perspectives and expertise that are invaluable in identifying and managing risks.

v. Provide Risk Awareness and Training
Creating awareness about risk management and providing relevant training to employees and stakeholders is essential. Training programs help develop risk management skills and ensure a risk-aware culture within the organization.

vi. Encourage Reporting of Risks and Near-Misses
Organizations should establish a culture that encourages employees to report potential risks and near-miss incidents. A non-punitive reporting culture helps in proactively identifying potential risks and implementing preventive measures.

vii. Utilize Technology
Technology plays a significant role in improving

communication and collaboration in risk management. Tools such as video conferencing, instant messaging, and project management software enable stakeholders to communicate and collaborate effectively, regardless of their location. Real-time monitoring and reporting of risks provide timely information for informed decision-making.

viii. Tailor Communication to the Audience
Understanding the audience and tailoring messages to their knowledge levels, attitudes, and concerns is crucial. Clear and concise messages, delivered through appropriate channels, ensure maximum impact and engagement.

Effective communication in risk management is not just about delivering information; it is about ensuring that the information is understood, acted upon, and leads to a coordinated effort in managing risks. By establishing clear communication channels, fostering open communication, involving stakeholders, providing training, encouraging reporting, utilizing technology, and tailoring messages to the audience, organizations can significantly enhance their risk management processes and outcomes.

o. Prioritize and Assess Risks
Prioritizing and assessing risks is a critical best practice in modern risk management for businesses. This process allows organizations to focus their limited resources on the most significant threats and opportunities, ensuring efficient and effective risk mitigation efforts.

To prioritize and assess risks effectively, businesses should follow these key steps:
   i. Evaluate impact and likelihood: For each identified risk, assess its potential impact on the organization's objectives and the likelihood of its occurrence. This evaluation should consider financial, operational, reputational, and strategic implications.
   ii. Use risk matrices: Employ visual tools like risk matrices to represent the impact and likelihood of risks. These matrices typically use color-coding to quickly identify high-priority risks, guiding decision-makers in their focus.
   iii. Conduct scenario analysis: Explore different potential

outcomes and their associated risks through scenario planning. Assign probability weights to various scenarios, emphasizing those with higher likelihood and impact during the prioritization process.

iv. Align with business objectives: Ensure that risk prioritization aligns with organizational goals and strategic objectives. Focus on risks that could impact critical business processes or disrupt key operations.

v. Quantify risks: Whenever possible, quantify risks in terms of their potential financial impact and probability. This quantification helps in comparing and ranking risks more objectively.

vi. Consider risk interdependencies: Assess how different risks may interact or compound each other, as this can affect their overall priority and impact.

vii. Involve stakeholders: Engage relevant stakeholders from various departments in the risk assessment process to gain diverse perspectives and ensure comprehensive evaluation.

viii. Use a consistent rating system: Develop and apply a consistent rating system for impact and likelihood across all identified risks to ensure fair comparison and prioritization.

ix. Regularly review and update: Risk prioritization should be an ongoing process. Regularly review and update risk assessments to reflect changes in the business environment, emerging threats, and evolving organizational objectives.

x. Leverage technology: Utilize risk management software and tools to streamline the prioritization process, enhance data analysis, and provide real-time insights into risk profiles.

By implementing these practices, businesses can create a more focused and effective risk management strategy. This approach allows organizations to allocate resources efficiently, addressing the most critical risks first while maintaining awareness of lower-priority threats. Ultimately, prioritizing and assessing risks enables businesses to make informed decisions, enhance resilience, and capitalize on opportunities in an increasingly complex and uncertain business landscape.

p. Implement a Quality Assurance Program
Implementing a Quality Assurance (QA) program is a crucial best practice for modern risk management in business. A well-designed QA program helps organizations maintain high standards, reduce errors, and mitigate risks associated with product or service quality. Here's an explanation of how to implement an effective QA program:
   i. Define Clear Objectives and Criteria
   The first step in implementing a QA program is to establish clear quality objectives and criteria. This involves identifying key performance indicators (KPIs) that align with your business goals and customer expectations. By setting specific, measurable targets, you create a foundation for evaluating and improving quality across your organization.
   ii. Develop Standardized Procedures
   Create scalable standardization procedures to ensure consistency in your quality assurance efforts. This includes documenting processes, workflows, and best practices that all employees should follow. Standardization helps reduce variability and makes it easier to identify and address quality issues.
   iii. Implement a Robust Feedback System
   Customer feedback is a critical component of any QA program. Distribute customer satisfaction surveys to gather insights on product or service quality, identify recurring issues, and prioritize areas for improvement. This feedback loop helps you stay aligned with customer needs and expectations.
   iv. Invest in Training and Coaching
   Focus on agent coaching and continuous improvement. Provide regular training sessions to keep your team updated on quality standards and best practices. Encourage a collaborative approach where employees are involved in the QA process, fostering a culture of quality throughout the organization.
   v. Utilize Technology and Data Analytics
   Implement a Computerized Maintenance Management System (CMMS) or similar technology to streamline your

QA processes. These tools can help you maintain accurate records, track performance metrics, and identify trends. Leverage data analytics to gain insights into quality issues and make data-driven decisions for improvement.

vi. Conduct Regular Audits and Calibration
Perform regular quality audits to ensure compliance with established standards. Additionally, conduct calibration sessions to ensure that feedback is reliable, consistent, and impartial across all evaluators. This helps maintain the integrity of your QA program and ensures that all team members are aligned on quality expectations.

vii. Focus on High-Value Interactions
While random sampling is important, pay special attention to high-value interactions or processes. This targeted approach allows you to assess performance in critical areas that have the most significant impact on your business and customer satisfaction.

viii. Continuous Improvement
Treat your QA program as an ongoing process rather than a one-time implementation. Regularly review and refine your quality objectives, procedures, and metrics based on changing business needs and customer expectations.

By implementing these best practices, businesses can create a robust Quality Assurance program that not only manages risks effectively but also drives continuous improvement and customer satisfaction. Remember that a successful QA program requires commitment from all levels of the organization and should be viewed as an investment in long-term success rather than a cost.

q. Leverage Data and Analytics
Leveraging data and analytics has become a crucial best practice for modern risk management in business. By harnessing the power of data-driven insights, organizations can significantly enhance their ability to identify, assess, and mitigate risks effectively.

One of the primary benefits of leveraging data and analytics in risk management is the ability to identify risks more accurately and comprehensively. By analyzing large volumes of data from various sources, businesses can uncover patterns, trends, and potential threats that may not be apparent through traditional risk assessment methods. This data-driven approach allows organizations to create a more holistic view of their risk landscape, including emerging risks that might otherwise go unnoticed.

Data analytics also enables businesses to conduct more sophisticated risk analysis. Advanced techniques such as Monte Carlo simulations, scenario planning, and sensitivity analysis can be applied to better understand the likelihood and potential consequences of various risk events. These analytical tools provide risk managers with a deeper understanding of the complex relationships between different risk factors and their potential impacts on business objectives.

Furthermore, leveraging data and analytics allows for more effective risk evaluation and prioritization. By quantifying risks based on historical data and predictive models, organizations can make more informed decisions about which risks require immediate attention and resources. This data-driven approach helps businesses allocate their risk management efforts more efficiently, focusing on the most critical areas of concern.

Real-time monitoring and analysis of risk indicators is another significant advantage of data-driven risk management. By continuously collecting and analyzing data, businesses can detect early warning signs of potential risks and respond more quickly to emerging threats. This proactive approach enables organizations to implement preventive measures or adjust their strategies before risks materialize into significant problems.

Predictive analytics plays a crucial role in modern risk management by allowing businesses to anticipate future trends and events based on historical data. By leveraging predictive models, organizations can forecast potential risks and their impacts, enabling them to develop more effective contingency plans and risk mitigation strategies.

Data visualization tools are also essential in communicating risk information effectively across the organization. By presenting complex risk data in easily understandable formats such as dashboards and interactive charts, risk managers can better engage stakeholders and facilitate more informed decision-making at all levels of the business.

To successfully leverage data and analytics for risk management, organizations should focus on several key areas:

i. Data quality and integration: Ensure that data from various sources is accurate, consistent, and properly integrated to provide a comprehensive view of the risk landscape.
ii. Advanced analytics capabilities: Invest in tools and expertise to perform sophisticated risk analysis, including predictive modeling and machine learning techniques.
iii. Cross-functional collaboration: Foster collaboration between risk management, data science, and business units to ensure that data-driven insights are effectively translated into actionable risk management strategies.
iv. Continuous monitoring and improvement: Implement systems for ongoing data collection and analysis to adapt risk management practices as new information becomes available.
v. Data governance and security: Establish robust data governance frameworks and security measures to protect sensitive risk-related information and ensure compliance with relevant regulations.

By adopting these best practices and leveraging data and analytics effectively, businesses can significantly enhance their risk management capabilities, leading to more resilient operations and better-informed strategic decisions in today's complex and rapidly changing business environment.

r. Collaborate Across Functions
In today's complex and interconnected business environment, effective risk management requires more than just isolated efforts from individual departments.

Cross-functional collaboration has emerged as a critical best practice for modern risk management, enabling organizations to leverage diverse expertise, streamline processes, and enhance overall resilience.

Benefits of Cross-Functional Collaboration
  i. Enhanced Knowledge Sharing
     Cross-functional collaboration breaks down silos, allowing for the free flow of information and knowledge across departments. This ensures that all team members have access to the most current and relevant data, which is crucial for identifying and mitigating risks effectively.
  ii. Accelerated Innovation
     By bringing together diverse perspectives and expertise, cross-functional teams can drive innovation more rapidly. This collaborative approach helps in developing creative solutions to complex problems, which is essential for staying ahead in a competitive market.
  iii. Improved Communication and Teamwork
     Effective cross-functional collaboration fosters stronger communication and teamwork. It encourages employees to understand and appreciate the roles and responsibilities of their colleagues, leading to a more cohesive and motivated workforce.
  iv. Streamlined Processes
     Collaboration across functions helps in identifying and eliminating redundant processes, thereby streamlining operations. This not only improves efficiency but also reduces the likelihood of errors and oversights that could lead to significant risks.
  v. Holistic Risk Management
     A cross-functional approach to risk management ensures that risks are viewed and addressed from multiple angles. This holistic perspective is vital for developing comprehensive risk mitigation strategies that consider all potential impacts on the organization.

Best Practices for Cross-Functional Collaboration
  i. Develop a Modern Collaboration Framework
     Establish a flexible and agile framework that supports real-time information sharing and decision-making. Utilize modern knowledge management platforms to connect team members and facilitate seamless communication.
  ii. Implement Unified Communication Tools
     Use integrated communication platforms that enable real-

time data sharing and collaboration. Tools like Slack, Teams, and project management software such as Asana or Trello can help in coordinating efforts and tracking progress efficiently.

iii. Provide Cross-Functional Training

Regular training sessions that focus on enhancing understanding of different departmental functions and protocols can bridge knowledge gaps and foster a collaborative culture. This is particularly important in areas like security operations, where coordinated efforts are crucial for effective incident response.

iv. Conduct Joint Simulations and Drills

Organize collaborative simulations and drills to practice responses to various risk scenarios. This helps in building a cohesive response strategy and ensures that all team members are prepared to act swiftly and effectively during actual incidents.

v. Establish Clear Communication Channels

Ensure that there are well-defined communication channels for sharing insights, challenges, and ideas. Encourage open dialogue and regular feedback to maintain transparency and continuous improvement.

vi. Align Goals and Objectives

Create a shared vision and align departmental goals to foster a collaborative mindset. This helps in uniting teams towards common objectives and ensures that all efforts are directed towards achieving the organization's strategic goals.

Cross-functional collaboration is a powerful strategy for modern risk management in business. By leveraging the collective expertise and resources of various departments, organizations can enhance their ability to identify, assess, and mitigate risks. Implementing best practices such as developing a modern collaboration framework, using unified communication tools, and providing cross-functional training can significantly improve the effectiveness of risk management efforts. Embracing this collaborative approach not only strengthens organizational resilience but also drives innovation and operational efficiency.

s. Conduct Scenario Planning
Scenario planning is a critical best practice for modern risk management in business, enabling organizations to navigate uncertainties and prepare for various potential futures. This approach involves creating multiple scenarios that represent different possible future states, allowing businesses to develop strategies to address each one effectively.

What is Scenario Planning?
Scenario planning is a strategic tool used to anticipate and prepare for potential future events and their impacts on an organization. Unlike traditional forecasting methods that often rely on linear projections of past trends, scenario planning considers a range of possible futures, including best-case, worst-case, and most-likely scenarios. This method helps organizations to be better prepared for unexpected changes and disruptions by envisioning various outcomes and developing corresponding strategies.

Importance in Modern Risk Management
   i. Enhancing Decision-Making
       Scenario planning empowers organizations to make informed decisions by considering multiple potential futures. This approach reduces the element of surprise and allows businesses to act swiftly and confidently when faced with unforeseen events. By preparing for various scenarios, companies can optimize their resources and make strategic decisions that align with their long-term goals and mission.
   ii. Mitigating Risks
       One of the primary benefits of scenario planning is its ability to mitigate risks. By simulating different disruptions and testing their impacts, organizations can identify vulnerabilities and develop contingency plans. This proactive approach helps in minimizing the adverse effects of unexpected events, such as natural disasters, political instability, or supply chain disruptions.
   iii. Driving Innovation and Strategic Transformation
       Scenario planning is not just a risk management tool but also a driver of innovation and strategic transformation. By exploring various future possibilities, organizations can

identify new opportunities and adapt their strategies to stay competitive. This forward-thinking approach encourages businesses to innovate and transform their operations to meet future challenges.

How to Conduct Scenario Planning

i. Identify Key Drivers and Uncertainties

The first step in scenario planning is to identify the key drivers and uncertainties that could impact the organization. These may include economic trends, technological advancements, regulatory changes, and market dynamics. Understanding these factors helps in creating realistic and relevant scenarios.

ii. Develop Multiple Scenarios

Next, organizations should develop multiple scenarios that represent different potential futures. These scenarios should cover a range of possibilities, from optimistic to pessimistic outcomes. Each scenario should be detailed, outlining the specific conditions and events that could occur.

iii. Analyze Impacts and Develop Strategies

Once the scenarios are developed, organizations need to analyze their potential impacts on various aspects of the business, such as operations, finances, and supply chains. Based on this analysis, they can develop strategies and action plans to address each scenario. This may involve creating contingency plans, diversifying supply sources, or investing in new technologies.

iv. Monitor and Update Scenarios

Scenario planning is an ongoing process that requires regular monitoring and updating. As new information and trends emerge, organizations should revisit their scenarios and adjust their strategies accordingly. This ensures that the business remains agile and prepared for any changes in the external environment.

Conducting scenario planning is a best practice for modern risk management in business. It enables organizations to anticipate and prepare for various potential futures, enhancing decision-making, mitigating risks, and driving innovation. By regularly updating their scenarios and strategies, businesses can stay resilient and competitive in an ever-changing world.

t. Continuously Improve and Adapt
Continuous improvement and adaptation are crucial components of modern risk management strategies in business. This approach enables organizations to stay ahead of emerging threats, optimize their risk mitigation efforts, and maintain resilience in an ever-changing business landscape.

To effectively implement continuous improvement and adaptation in risk management, organizations should focus on several key practices:
   i. Regular risk assessments: Conduct frequent and comprehensive risk assessments to identify new threats and evaluate the effectiveness of existing controls. This process should involve reviewing past incidents, analyzing trends, and consulting with stakeholders to uncover emerging risks.
   ii. Robust risk monitoring: Establish a robust risk monitoring system to detect changes in the risk environment. This includes tracking internal and external factors that could impact the business, such as regulatory changes, market shifts, or geopolitical events.
   iii. Scenario planning: Develop hypothetical scenarios that could affect the business and assess their potential impact. This practice helps organizations prepare for a range of possible outcomes and adjust their risk management strategies accordingly.
   iv. Embrace technology: Leverage advanced technologies such as data analytics and artificial intelligence to enhance risk management capabilities. These tools can help identify emerging risks, analyze trends, and streamline the risk management process.
   v. Foster a culture of learning and innovation: Encourage employees to embrace new ideas, experiment with different approaches, and learn from failures. This culture of continuous learning and innovation can significantly enhance an organization's ability to adapt to new challenges and improve risk management practices.

vi. Conduct regular reviews and updates: Continuously review and update risk management policies, procedures, and strategies. This ensures that the organization's approach remains relevant and effective in addressing current and future risks.
vii. Encourage cross-functional collaboration: Break down silos within the organization and promote collaboration across different departments. This approach allows for a more holistic view of risks and enables the development of more comprehensive risk management strategies.
viii. Stay informed about industry trends: Actively monitor industry trends, market shifts, and emerging technologies to anticipate potential challenges and adapt strategies accordingly. This proactive approach allows organizations to stay ahead of potential risks and seize new opportunities.
ix. Benchmark against industry best practices: Compare your risk management practices with those of industry leaders and adopt proven strategies that align with your organization's goals.
x. Invest in employee training: Provide ongoing training to ensure that employees are aware of the latest risks and mitigation strategies. This helps create a risk-aware culture throughout the organization.

By implementing these practices, organizations can create a dynamic and responsive risk management framework that evolves with the changing business environment. This approach not only helps mitigate potential threats but also positions the organization to capitalize on new opportunities that may arise from changing market conditions.

Continuous improvement and adaptation in risk management are not just about avoiding negative outcomes; they are about building organizational resilience and agility.

By consistently refining and updating their risk management strategies, businesses can enhance their decision-making processes, improve operational efficiency, and ultimately drive long-term success in an increasingly complex and uncertain world.

Chapter Conclusion:
By implementing these best practices, organizations can take a proactive, holistic approach to risk management that protects assets, builds stakeholder trust, and enhances operational resilience.

A proactive approach to risk management is essential for businesses to thrive in today's complex and uncertain environment.

16 Cheat book

Cheat book is something like a pocket book on what we have learned from this book. You may not find words, sentences, paragraphs, definition as same from the book here, but this is like a short summary to remember for your knowledge in exams or future reference.

Introduction

In today's complex and rapidly evolving business landscape, effective risk management has become a critical component of organizational success and sustainability.

Companies must navigate a wide array of risks, from financial and operational to strategic and reputational, in order to achieve their objectives and maintain a competitive edge.

This summary provides an overview of modern risk management practices, highlighting key concepts, strategies, and best practices that organizations can leverage to mitigate risks and capitalize on opportunities.

Fundamentals of Risk Management
Definition of Risk and Risk Management

Risk can be defined as the potential for an event or action to adversely impact an organization's ability to achieve its objectives. Risk management, on the other hand, is the process of identifying, assessing, and responding to risks in order to minimize their negative impact and maximize opportunities.

History and Evolution of Risk Management

Risk management practices have evolved significantly over time. Early risk management focused primarily on insurable risks, such as property damage and liability. However, as the business environment became more complex, risk management expanded to include a wider range of risks, including strategic, operational, and financial risks.

Risk Management Process

The risk management process typically involves four key steps: risk identification, risk assessment, risk response, and risk monitoring and control. Organizations use a variety of techniques, such as SWOT analysis, PESTLE analysis, and scenario planning, to identify and assess risks.

Benefits of Risk Management

Effective risk management can provide numerous benefits to organizations, including improved decision-making, reduced costs, enhanced reputation, and increased resilience in the face of unexpected events.

Types of Risks

Organizations face a wide range of risks, including strategic risks (e.g., competitive threats, technological disruption), operational risks (e.g., supply chain failures, human error), financial risks (e.g., market volatility, credit risk), compliance risks (e.g., regulatory changes, legal disputes), security and fraud risks (e.g., cyber-attacks, internal fraud), and reputational risks (e.g., negative publicity, stakeholder dissatisfaction).

Risk Identification and Assessment

Risk Identification Techniques

Organizations use a variety of techniques to identify risks, including SWOT analysis (identifying strengths, weaknesses, opportunities, and threats), PESTLE analysis (examining political, economic, social, technological, legal, and environmental factors), brainstorming, scenario analysis, bow-tie analysis, risk checklists, and interviews and surveys.

Risk Assessment Methods

Once risks have been identified, organizations assess their likelihood and potential impact using qualitative and quantitative methods. Qualitative methods include risk heat maps and probability and impact matrices, while quantitative methods involve statistical analysis and modeling. Leveraging technology and data can enhance risk assessment capabilities.

Risk Mitigation Strategies

Organizations can employ a range of strategies to mitigate risks, including risk acceptance (accepting the risk and its consequences), risk avoidance (eliminating the risk by avoiding the activity), risk transfer (transferring the risk to a third party, such as through insurance), risk reduction (implementing controls and safeguards to reduce the likelihood and impact of risks), and risk sharing (sharing the risk with partners or stakeholders).

Other risk mitigation strategies include risk buffering (maintaining reserves or contingency plans to absorb the impact of risks), risk strategizing (incorporating risk considerations into strategic decision-making), risk testing (conducting simulations and stress tests to assess the effectiveness of risk controls), risk quantification (assigning monetary values to risks), risk digitization (leveraging technology to automate and optimize risk management processes), risk diversification (spreading risks across different activities or locations), and implementing controls and safeguards (such as policies, procedures, and systems to mitigate risks).

Risk Monitoring and Reporting

Effective risk management requires ongoing monitoring and reporting to ensure that risks are being managed effectively and that new risks are identified and addressed in a timely manner. Organizations establish key risk indicators (KRIs) to monitor risk levels, develop risk dashboards to visualize and communicate risk information, implement incident reporting systems to capture and analyze risk events, conduct continuous monitoring and auditing to assess the effectiveness of risk controls, and perform trend analysis to identify emerging risks and patterns.

Financial Risk Management

Financial risk management focuses on managing risks related to financial markets, such as credit risk (the risk of default by borrowers or counterparties), market risk (the risk of losses due to changes in market prices), liquidity risk (the risk of being unable to meet financial obligations), and operational risk (the risk of losses due to inadequate or failed internal processes, people, or systems). Hedging and derivatives are commonly used to mitigate financial risks.

Enterprise Risk Management (ERM)

Enterprise risk management (ERM) is a holistic approach to managing risks across an organization. ERM frameworks, such as the COSO ERM Framework and the ISO 31000 Risk Management Standard, provide guidance on integrating risk management into business strategy, establishing governance and leadership structures, building a risk-aware culture, and defining risk appetite and tolerance levels.

Regulatory and Compliance Risk

Regulatory and compliance risks arise from the need to adhere to laws, regulations, and industry standards. Organizations must understand and comply with relevant regulatory requirements, implement compliance programs, conduct internal audits, and manage risks related to anti-money laundering (AML) and data protection and privacy regulations.

Technology and Cyber Risk

Technology and cyber risks have become increasingly important in recent years, as organizations rely more heavily on digital systems and face growing threats from cyber-attacks and data breaches. Organizations must assess and manage cyber risks, develop data breach response plans, and leverage technology to enhance risk management capabilities.

Operational Risk Management

Operational risk management focuses on managing risks related to day-to-day business operations, such as business continuity planning, disaster recovery planning, crisis management, and supply chain risk management. Organizations must ensure that they can maintain critical operations and recover from disruptive events.

Strategic Risk Management

Strategic risk management involves identifying and managing risks that could impact an organization's ability to achieve its strategic objectives. Techniques include scenario planning, competitive risk analysis, assessing risks related to mergers and acquisitions, and managing risks associated with innovation.

Reputation Risk Management

Reputation risk management focuses on managing risks that could damage an organization's reputation and public image. This includes managing media and public relations, engaging with stakeholders, developing crisis communication plans, and mitigating risks related to social media.

Risk Management Tools and Software

Organizations can leverage a variety of tools and software to enhance their risk management capabilities, such as risk management information systems (RMIS) to centralize risk data and reporting, predictive analytics to identify and assess emerging risks, and specialized software for risk assessment and monitoring.

Case Studies

The book provides several case studies of organizations that have successfully implemented risk management practices, such as Intuit's enterprise risk management program and Walmart's approach to managing complex risks across its global operations.

Best Practices

The book highlights several best practices for effective risk management, including conducting regular risk assessments, investing in training and education for employees, establishing clear accountability for risk management, and committing to continuous improvement of risk management performance measurement and monitoring.

www.ingramcontent.com/pod-product-compliance
Lightning Source LLC
Chambersburg PA
CBHW071918210526
45479CB00002B/467